The Path to Universal Health Coverage in Bangladesh

A WORLD BANK STUDY

The Path to Universal Health Coverage in Bangladesh

Bridging the Gap of Human Resources for Health

Sameh El-Saharty, Susan Powers Sparkes, Helene Barroy, Karar Zunaid Ahsan, and Syed Masud Ahmed

WORLD BANK GROUP

Contents

Boxes

Figures

Tables

Preface

In 2011, Japan celebrated the 50th anniversary of achieving universal health coverage (UHC). To mark the occasion, the government of Japan and the World Bank conceived the idea of undertaking a multicountry study to respond to this growing demand by sharing rich and varied country experiences from countries at different stages of adopting and implementing strategies for UHC, including Japan itself. This led to the formation of a joint Japan–World Bank research team under the Japan–World Bank Partnership Program for Universal Health Coverage. The Program was set up as a two-year multicountry study to help fill the gap in knowledge about the policy decisions and implementation processes that countries undertake when they adopt the UHC goals. The Program was funded through the generous support of the government of Japan. This Country Study on Bangladesh is one of the 11 country studies on UHC that was commissioned under the Japan–World Bank Partnership Program. The other participating countries are Brazil, Ethiopia, France, Ghana, Indonesia, Japan, Peru, Thailand, Turkey, and Vietnam.

Acknowledgments

This study was prepared by a World Bank team comprising Sameh El-Saharty, Senior Health Policy Specialist, World Bank; Susan Powers Sparkes, Health Economist, World Bank Consultant; Helene Barroy, Health Economist, World Bank; Karar Zunaid Ahsan, Senior Research Associate, MEASURE Evaluation, University of North Carolina at Chapel Hill; and Syed Masud Ahmed, Director, Centre of Excellence for Universal Health Coverage, ICDDR,B, Bangladesh.

The study benefited from two background papers prepared under a contract with BRAC University under the oversight of Dr. Tim Evans, then Dean of the James P. Grant School of Public Health, and Dr. Sadia Afroze Chowdhury, Executive Director of BRAC Institute of Global Health; these papers are *Overview of the Current State of the Health Workforce in Bangladesh* by Professor Syed Masud Ahmed, Director, Centre of Excellence for Universal Health Coverage, ICDDR,B and of the James P. Grant School of Public Health, and by Dr. M. A. Sabur, Independent Consultant; and *HRH Policy in Bangladesh: Evolution, Implementation and the Process* by Ferdous Arfina Osman, Ph.D., Professor, Department of Public Administration, Dhaka University. Appendix C, "Economic Analysis for Options to Increase Health Care Providers by 2021," was prepared by Dr. Lung Vu, Economist and World Bank Consultant.

The study benefited from useful comments and feedback from the officials of the Ministry of Health and Family Welfare, Government of Bangladesh, including Md. Ashadul Islam, Director General, Health Economics Unit (HEU); and Md. Hafizur Ramhan, Director (Research), HEU.

The study was peer reviewed by Aparnaa Somanathan, Senior Health Economist; Edson Correia Araujo, Health Economist; and Christopher H. Herbst, Health Specialist, Health, Nutrition, and Population Global Practice at the World Bank. The study was reviewed and discussed in a meeting chaired by Mr. Johannes Zutt, Country Director for Bangladesh, Bhutan and Nepal at the World Bank.

Useful comments were also provided by the Bangladesh Health Team including Albertus Voetberg, Lead Health Specialist; Somil Nagpal, Senior Health Specialist; and Iffat Mahmud, Operations Officer.

The study was edited by Jonathan Aspin and Shazia Amin, World Bank Consultants.

Executive Summary

As part of its commitment to achieving universal health coverage (UHC) by 2032—announced by Prime Minister Sheikh Hasina at the 64th World Health Assembly in May 2011—the government of Bangladesh is exploring policy options to mobilize additional financial resources for health and to expand coverage while improving service quality and availability. To succeed, it will have to reform its service delivery systems, as well as its own internal policy making. From a service delivery perspective, the country faces particularly critical challenges in its health workforce, and so human resources for health (HRH) will need to be a focus of any initiative to achieve UHC.

The country faces multiple challenges in its efforts to achieve UHC by 2032; these are analyzed under the rubrics of HRH and HRH policy challenges. Some policy options are then posited.

HRH

The main challenges are as follows:

Shortages. Bangladesh is experiencing an extreme health workforce crisis. As of 2007, there were only around five physicians and two nurses per 10,000 population (Ahmed, Hossain et al. 2011), with particular shortages in hard-to-reach areas (Government of Bangladesh 2012a). Even with the growth in training institutions (see below), absolute shortages of health workers will continue in the coming years. Shortages stem from low public sector salaries (the entry-level salary is inadequate for a family of five, a common family size), inadequate HRH production, combined with migration, inordinately slow recruitment, and difficulty in staff retention, particularly in remote areas.

Production Shortfalls. While the number of institutes and places ("seats") have been increasing recently, the trend of production is unlikely to fulfill the gaps, whether in numbers or health needs. And the total number of seats for doctors continues to be more than double those for nurses, thus perpetuating the skewed doctor-to-nurse ratio.

High Vacancy Rates and Slow Recruitment. Of all sanctioned public posts for doctors, 27 percent remain unfilled; more widely, 20 percent of the 115,530 posts under the Directorate General of Health Services (DGHS) are vacant

(DGHS 2012)—and some have been vacant for years. The vacancy litany continues: 21.0 percent of posts for medical technologists, 9.0 percent for mid-level staff, and 13.4 percent in nursing services. This high number of vacancies stems largely from the length of recruitment (the entire process—from identification of a vacancy to final hiring—can take up to three years in the public sector, partly because several government bodies are involved). The issue is compounded by staff absenteeism, mainly of doctors and nurses, which may range from 7.5 to 40 percent on any particular day (Chaudhury and Hammer 2004; Bangladesh Health Facility Survey 2012). The hard-to-reach areas have far worse vacancy rates than the above national figures, as most workers want to live and work in major urban metropolitan areas—one of the major factors in the inequitable distribution of health staff in Bangladesh.

Skill-Mix Imbalances. Crucially, the nurse-to-doctor ratio is the reverse of the World Health Organization (WHO) recommendation of three nurses for one physician, with more than two doctors in practice for every one nurse (Ahmed, Hossain et al. 2011). In 2011, doctors made up 70 percent of the total registered professional workforce; the remaining 30 percent were support staff (Government of Bangladesh 2012a).

Urban and Gender Biases. The heavy urban bias in the government health workforce has been an issue since independence (Ahmed, Hossain et al. 2011), and governments have persistently failed to resolve it. Fewer than 20 percent of HRH are providing services to more than 75 percent of the rural population. The doctor-to-population ratio is 1:1,500 in urban areas, but 10 times worse in rural areas—1:15,000 (Mabud 2005). Despite commitments of various government plans to rectify wide geographic imbalances, they remain, partly because the underlying factors have not been resolved. There are, for example, no incentives for posting and retaining health workers in remote and hard-to-reach areas (Government of Bangladesh 2008). There are also higher vacancy rates and lower numbers of female health workers in rural areas, exacerbating matters. Gender imbalance also persists in staffing patterns, as the majority of doctors, dentists, technicians, and pharmacists are male (the majority of nurses are female).

Quality of Health Care Provision and Productivity of Health Care Providers (HCPs). Although poor quality of provision comes across in studies, there is no systematic process to assess quality of medical care, whether in public or private sectors. Findings from a few small-scale studies indicate that there is significant room to improve the technical quality of care provided by them (Arifeen et al. 2005; Chowdhury, Hossain, and Halim 2009; Hasan 2012). Studies also show that nurses spend only a small fraction of their duty times on patient care, sometimes as low as 5 percent in government hospitals (for example, Hadley et al. 2007). The main reasons are societal norms related to stigmatization and low status of the profession, which lead to nurses in government hospitals trying to distance themselves from patients.

Work Environment. Beyond the fact that the shortage of workers leads to excess workloads, factors undermining health worker morale include inadequate supply of drugs and equipment, weak administrative support, dual-job holding, lack of scope for career progression, limited in-service training opportunities, and restrictive civil service incentive structures (especially for nurses)—all contributing to skilled health workers leaving the profession or migrating to other countries.

HRH Policy Challenges

The policy-making environment is weak and characterized by the following challenges:

A Complex Array of National Policies. Bangladesh's complex and sometimes contradictory array of national policies have had mixed results since the early 1970s. Despite the efforts and some successes, the problems that still characterize HRH highlight the government's inability to tackle HRH-related challenges. Policy making is also subject to the political influence of stakeholder and interest groups that can result in a lack of strategic planning and misaligned priorities.

A Highly Centralized and Cumbersome Bureaucratic System with Weak Response Capacity. The overly cumbersome, bureaucratic, and centralized system leaves space for different stakeholder groups to exert their influence at a number of different points in policy making. This system also makes it difficult for the Ministry of Health and Family Welfare (MOHFW) to effectively implement reforms to the health workforce due to the multiple government entities required to sign off on any policy changes. This burdensome system does not provide for clear lines of accountability, resulting in a low capacity to both implement and enforce policy reforms. For example, to establish a new post in the MOHFW six ministries or institutional entities are involved until final approval, taking anywhere from six months to two years. Similarly, filling a physician vacancy (once established in the public sector) can take up to three years, due in part to the multiple government bodies involved.

A Range of Powerful Stakeholders, Some with Competing Interests. These include physicians, who as policy setters have ensured a constant push to increase the number of doctors relative to other health workers, so that the country now has far too many doctors relative to the number of nurses; politicians, whose pre-election promises may divert resources from more pressing policies; development partners, whose resources constituted 7.2 percent of total health expenditure (THE) in 2012 (WHO 2014) may not be entirely aligned with the MOHFW priorities; and nurses, other health workers, and informal providers (although they have relatively little power in the system, despite constituting 88 percent of all HCPs) (Ahmed et al. 2009).

Weak Regulatory and Enforcement Capacity, Contributing to High Rates of Absenteeism and Many Unqualified Health Workers. Due to the factors discussed above, the MOHFW has been unable to put into place regulations that allow for the full implementation of important policies. For instance, despite efforts to increase rural retention and place health workers in remote and hard-to-reach areas, the urban bias of the distribution of health workers persists. This distribution is then exacerbated by high rates of absenteeism in rural areas. The MOHFW is aware of these issues, but has been unable to effectively monitor or enforce policies to address them. Another example is the MOHFW's inability to stem the pervasive use and presence of unqualified health workers by Bangladeshis. As of 2007, informal sector providers constituted 88 percent of all HCPs in the country (Ahmed et al. 2009). These unqualified providers are the primary source of health care for Bangladeshis in some remote areas of the country (Mahmood et al. 2010).

HRH Policy Options for UHC

To reach its goal of UHC by 2032, the government will have to commit itself to policies to strengthen its health workforce. Below are different policy options to address some of the key HRH challenges for the government to consider:

Address HRH Shortages

The following strategies may help reduce the HRH shortage:

Accelerate filling current vacancies. The first step in addressing the shortage of HCPs is to fill currently available and vacant positions where HCP supply is sufficient. The MOHFW needs to engage other ministries and local authorities to improve coordination and the overall hiring process. For its part, the MOHFW also needs to focus on improving efficiency in the hiring process.

Accelerate the recruitment of nurses and community health workers (CHWs), and introduce a comprehensive HRH master plan. A modeling exercise assessed the feasibility of different HCP scaling-up scenarios and generated three possible scenarios that use 100 percent of the potential fiscal threshold available for physicians, nurses, and CHWs, but each scenario aims at achieving a different physician: nurse: CHW ratio (appendix C). Scenario II is probably the most feasible as it will absorb almost all graduates of nursing schools and achieve a physician: nurse: CHW ratio of 1:1.5:1 by 2021. To accelerate closing the gap, the current sector-wide approach (SWAp) may be a vehicle for financing the recruitment of nurses and CHWs until budget resources are available. In addition, the MOHFW needs to have a master plan for HRH to guide the recruitment of new HCPs, which can be based on the modeling detailed in appendix C.

Make working in the public sector more attractive. The MOHFW, with the Ministry of Finance and Ministry of Public Administration, should consider using financial and nonfinancial incentives to attract health workers into the public sector. Incentive structures and performance bonuses should be carefully assessed to ensure that remuneration levels are appropriately set to entice HCPs into the public health sector.

Explore contracting mechanisms with nonstate service providers. The MOHFW should explore contracting mechanisms with nonstate providers to supplement the public HCP network to meet the expected increased demand from expanding health coverage. It already has experience in contracting nongovernmental organizations (NGOs) for nutrition and human immunodeficiency virus/acquired immune deficiency syndrome (HIV/AIDS) services, which can be built on to strengthen the contract management function. A relevant example is Afghanistan's strategy to form partnerships with NGOs, which has led to higher quality of care for the poor (Hansen et al. 2008).

Regulate dual practice for public sector health workers. The MOHFW needs to take steps to regulate and enforce dual practice norms. With 80 percent of all public sector physicians engaged in dual practice, there is potential for misuse of the system (ICDDR,B 2010). Turkey was successful in reducing the proportion of physicians engaged in dual practice through a mixture of financial incentives and stricter enforcement of regulations (Evans 2013; Vujicic et al. 2009).

Engage other government entities to expedite the hiring process. Nine government entities are involved in recruiting public sector employees. The MOHFW needs to engage in a dialogue at cabinet level to highlight the HRH crisis and its impact on impeding the prime minister's vision for UHC and for the Public Service Commission to give priority and expedite hiring of HCPs. The government should also reevaluate its mandatory retirement age of 59 for all public sector workers, as it is losing experienced providers.

Establish high-level coordination platforms in the MOHFW. The MOHFW should implement the planned National Health Workforce Committee and National Professional Standards Committee as laid out in the Health Workforce Strategy for 2012–32. These entities should be responsible for leading the coordinated effort to train, recruit, deploy, and regulate all HCPs in the country, so as to set workload standards that should increase the role of nurses, midwives, and paraprofessionals. Successful strategies in other countries include a bundle of interventions, including greater social and community support, embedded within broader multisector development actions, as in Chile, Indonesia, Thailand, and Zambia (Lehmann, Dieleman, and Martineau 2008; Peña et al. 2010).

Improve the Skill-Mix
The MOHFW needs to reverse the current ratio of 2.5 physicians for every nurse and midwife. Strategies should include the following:

• ***Introduce task shifting.*** As recruitment for physicians is slow, task shifting of some of the doctors' tasks to other HCPs would be a viable option. Auxiliary HCPs like CHWs, nurse aids, traditional birth attendants, and medical assistants are an integral part of health systems in many national health systems including Malawi, Tanzania, Ghana, Argentina, Brazil, Ethiopia, and Mozambique (Araujo and Maeda 2013). This would require a careful assessment of the current workload of existing HCPs with tools such as the WHO's Workload Indicators of Staffing Needs process (WHO 2010a). The MOHFW needs to work with the Bangladesh Medical Association and the Nursing Association to carve out specific tasks that nurses can take on.

- *Improve the stature of nurses and midwives.* Social stigma against treatment by nurses and midwives can be reduced by informing the public of the vital role they play. A public education campaign is needed to promote and improve the stature of nurses and midwives, which should increase demand for training. Another effective approach to promote the status of different health care cadres, as seen in Cuba, is the government's active role in training and exporting of health professionals to other countries (Reed 2010).
- *Increase production capacity for nurses.* To achieve a better skill-mix of doctor-to-nurse ratio of 1:2 (scenario III, appendix C), the existing production capacity of nurses needs to be increased by 10 percent a year for the next 10 years. The rationale for this policy includes the following: the cost per nurse is only half that of the doctor (World Bank 2003); nurses are more likely to work in rural areas (Bangladesh Health Watch 2008); and there are positive correlations between the nurse-to-physician ratio and health outcomes (Ahmed, Hossain et al. 2011; Bigbee 2008). In Bangladesh, Khulna is the only division where there is a higher nurse-to-physician ratio and is showing better health service utilization and health outcome indicators.
- *Create new cadres of community skilled birth attendants and midwives.* The MOHFW should train new health workers as community skilled birth attendants and midwives, and not only pull from the existing health workforce to fill these roles. Evidence from Afghanistan demonstrates how new cadres of nurses and midwives contribute in rebuilding the primary care and emergency services (Acerra et al. 2009) and in increasing skilled birth attendance (Mohmand 2013).
- *Use CHWs to supplement formal HCPs.* The MOHFW should train and use CHWs to provide basic services and act as an extension of the formal health sector and should be considered an integral part of the health system. This can build on the successful example of the effective use of CHWs for tuberculosis (TB) control and treatment under Bangladesh Rural Advancement Committee (BRAC) (May, Rhatigan, and Cash 2011).

Address Geographic Imbalances

There are several strategies to improve the rural–urban distribution of HCPs. First strategy is to introduce targeted training programs for community and traditional health workers. The MOHFW should train informal sector health workers since they are the primary point of contact with the health system for many Bangladeshis in rural areas (Mahmood et al. 2010). Targeted training activities have been shown to be effective in Bangladesh (Hamid, Roberts, and Mosley 2011; Sarma and Oliveras 2011). However, this should be done in regions that suffer from extreme shortages of HCPs and only for a limited time until enough qualified HCPs are mobilized. Second strategy is to establish regional training institutions. The MOHFW needs to create training institutions in rural areas and use careful examination requirements for rural trainees to maximize the likelihood of their staying in these areas once they complete training. By placing institutions in these rural areas and recruiting from local populations, trainees may be more likely to practice there as HCPs, as seen in countries like China, the Democratic Republic of Congo, Japan, and the United States (Dolea, Stormont, and Braichet 2010; WHO 2010a). In addition, the MOHFW should design continuing education and professional development programs that meet the needs of rural health workers (WHO 2010a). Third is to implement mandatory service requirements. The current mandatory service requirements in the public sector should be expanded and enforced. Rural service should also be required for professional licensing. Such interventions are in place in more than 70 countries (Frehywot et al. 2010). Finally, the MOHFW should consider introducing targeted recruitment practices. The MOHFW should use targeted recruitment policies to increase the likelihood of retention in rural areas (WHO 2010a). As suggested in the study scenario II (detailed in appendix C) is probably the most feasible for increasing the number of HCPs, and detailed deployment data under this scenario are in table 5.4. To improve geographic distribution, most nurses and CHWs will be deployed to Sylhet, Rajshahi, and Barisal.

Retain Health Workers

Health workers must be retained by the health system, entailing a raft of strategies. A first step for the MOHFW to increase numbers of health workers is to draw health workers employed in the nonhealth sector back into the health sector through financial and nonfinancial incentives. At the same time, there is a need to establish a placement system for trainees. A pipeline for trainees should be created while they are still in school so they can immediately enter public health service, without recruitment delays. The MOHFW should work with training institutions to identify these candidates and ensure their placement. In addition, the MOHFW should create a clear career development system. The MOHFW should unify the career progression pathways between different directorates, particularly for nurses to improve their retention, which will involve coordinated in-service training and differential pay grades. Finally, establishing a well-coordinated performance-based system can provide additional funds for HCPs to keep them in the public sector, particularly in underserved areas. For example, nonfinancial incentives have been shown to be effective in retaining CHWs in Bangladesh (Alam et al. 2012a, 2012b; Rahman et al. 2010). Several countries, including Thailand, Zambia, Mozambique, Kenya, and Chile, have taken initiatives to provide incentives outside the salaries and payments to improve retention, which include government housing to staff (Araujo and Maeda 2013). Performance incentives to practice in rural areas have been successful in retaining physicians in rural areas in Thailand (Tangcharoensathien et al. 2013).

Adopt Strategic Payment and Purchaser Mechanisms

Payment mechanisms should incentivize performance from both public and private sector providers. However, careful analysis will need to be conducted to set payment levels if these mechanisms are to be expanded to general health services. One potential source of additional revenues to pay providers is donor funds such as under a SWAp in Malawi (Carlson et al. 2008). Additionally, the private sector contracting mechanisms, such as those used in Turkey, may effectively fill gaps in public sector provision, particularly in rural and hard-to-reach areas to meet the increased demand as UHC is implemented.

Establish a Central Human Resources Information System

The MOHFW needs to establish a central Human Resources Information System (HRIS) to strengthen and coordinate with the existing director general–level personnel management and information systems to produce real-time human resources scenarios by geographic regions and to feed into the MOHFW's decision making and policy development. Without this coordinated and centralized system, the MOHFW's current endeavor to formulate its HRH strategy will not be implementable. This intervention has been shown to be effective in Peru, where a centralized HRIS led to strengthened stewardship of the MOHFW over human resources development (Dayrit et al. 2011).

Target HRH Interventions to Improve Maternal and Newborn Health

The MOHFW will have to engage in targeted interventions to improve HRH capacities in these areas. First, it should train and deploy all cadres of health personnel, including community-based skilled birth attendants, in teams to small facilities to meet the goal of increasing skilled birth attendant coverage by 30 percent by 2015. This approach would scale up access to these services 10 times faster than deploying individual health workers for home deliveries. Second, before increasing comprehensive emergency obstetric care (EmOC) facilities at upazila (subdistrict) and union levels, it may be more effective for the MOHFW to invest first in the 62 district and general hospitals and 22 medical colleges so they can provide comprehensive EmOC 24 hours a day, 7 days a week (Koblinsky et al. 2008).

Way Forward

To achieve UHC by 2032, the government will have to pursue policy reforms to mobilize additional financing for health and concurrently to address critical HRH shortages and distribution issues. More specifically, the government will need to improve rural retention of health workers, reverse skill-mix distribution ratios between physicians and other cadres of health workers, and improve newborn and maternal health in particular. An important starting point will be streamlining government recruitment and other HRH-related policies. Government processes, including establishing training institutions; developing curricula; and recruiting, transferring, and promoting staff, should be carefully examined. Efforts should be made across government entities to improve these systems. Finally, the government needs to invest resources to improve coordination and managerial capacity within government entities involved in designing and implementing policies.

Acronyms

BMA	Bangladesh Medical Association
BPL	Below poverty line
BRAC	Bangladesh Rural Advancement Committee
BSc	Bachelor of Science
CHW	Community health worker
CSBA	Community skilled birth attendant
DGHS	Directorate/Director General of Health Services
DGFP	Directorate General of Family Planning
DHS	Demographic and Health Survey
FWV	Family welfare visitor
HCP	Health care provider
HRH	Human resources for health
MBBS	Bachelor of Medicine and Bachelor of Surgery
MD	Doctor of Medicine
MOHFW	Ministry of Health and Family Welfare
NGO	Nongovernmental organization
NHP	National Health Policy
NIPORT	National Institute of Population Research and Training
NIPSOM	National Institute of Preventive and Social Medicine
PSC	Public Service Commission
SHPS	Social Health Protection Scheme
SWAp	Sector-wide approach
TBA	Traditional birth attendant
THE	Total health expenditure
UNDP	United Nations Development Programme
WHO	World Health Organization

All dollar amounts are US dollars unless otherwise indicated.

CHAPTER 1

Introduction

Overview

The government of Bangladesh, as part of its commitment to achieving universal health coverage (UHC) by 2032, is exploring policy options to mobilize additional financial resources for the health sector to expand coverage while improving service quality and availability. From a service delivery perspective, Bangladesh faces particularly critical challenges with respect to its health workforce. As a result, human resources for health (HRH) must be a focus of any policy initiative directed at achieving UHC.

The main objectives of this study are to assess the HRH status and policy making in Bangladesh and to provide policy options as to how decision makers can work to improve availability of health workers on the road toward achieving UHC. It seeks to ensure that the current commitment to achieving UHC in Bangladesh actually leads to effective health coverage for all Bangladeshis. In particular, it raises awareness of the critical problems facing the health workforce and the related policy processes.

The study is organized to first provide an overview of the government's planned path to UHC and the HRH status and related policies in Bangladesh. It then gives a detailed discussion of policy options related to improving availability and skill-mix of the health workforce. The study presents an overview of the government's planned path to UHC (chapter 2); an overview of the HRH situation and its key constraints (chapter 3); a review of HRH policy-making process (chapter 4); and proposed policy options (chapter 5).

Two Key Dates: 2021 and 2032

The year 2021 marks the 50th anniversary of national liberation and the establishment of the state of Bangladesh. By then the government aims to have taken the country to middle-income status (Government of Bangladesh 2012a).

The year 2032 is the date that Prime Minister Sheikh Hasina has set to achieve universal health coverage (UHC)—30 years from when this commitment was made.

Laudable goals—but are they achievable?

The answer would seem in the affirmative based on the following: Although a low-income country with a gross domestic product (GDP) per capita of only $840 in 2013 (World Bank 2013), in recent years, Bangladesh has made great strides in improving its economic and social development outcomes. This progress is particularly notable in the health sector, where it is on track to achieve most of its health-related Millennium Development Goal (MDG) targets. This is all the more impressive as it has spent only around 3.5 percent of GDP on health, one of the lowest rates in the region, while at the same time surpassing its neighbors in increasing life expectancy and in reducing fertility and the mortality rate of mothers and infants.

But against this, for example, stand emerging and reemerging infectious diseases (dengue, swine, and bird flu, for instance); mass arsenicosis; the emerging burden of noncommunicable diseases; very heavy rates of road traffic accidents; and mental health issues. All these require an adequate and quality health workforce as evidence exists that density of the health workers in a population is closely associated with substantial gains in health (Joint Learning Initiative [JLI] 2004).

Further, about one-third of the population is still poor (Bangladesh Bureau of Statistics [BBS] 2011), and health care costs (especially catastrophic) are a major contributor to this persistently high rate. A 2007 multicountry study estimated that the poverty head count was 3.8 percent higher than it would otherwise have been without households' medical expenditures (Van Doorslaer et al. 2007). Bangladesh is also undergoing a demographic transition as population growth slows and life expectancy increases. Replacement levels of fertility have been nearly reached, with a total fertility rate of about 2.2 children per woman in 2011 (World Bank 2012). These slowing fertility rates may end the country's population growth by midcentury. The result of this trend is a long-term demographic bulge of young people who will need jobs and elderly people who will need more expensive and prolonged medical care as they live longer.

This aging along with the epidemiological transition affect primarily poor populations, and only by expanding coverage and achieving UHC in the next couple of decades can Bangladesh effectively contain future health care costs and ensure equity in health care.

The country faces multiple challenges in its efforts to achieve UHC by 2032. One of the key challenges, HRH, is analyzed in detail in this study in terms of the status, distribution, skill-mix, and policy-making process. In the final chapter, this study explores some policy options for the government's consideration in addressing these challenges. First, though, it explores in more detail the key challenges—as a measure of what must be overcome.

Key Challenges

Bangladesh continues to suffer from a critical HRH crisis, which has several well-recognized factors. In addition to extreme shortages of all cadres of health workers, there are particularly acute skill-mix problems. In particular, the ratio of doctors to nurses is the reverse of that recommended by the World Health Organization (WHO), with more than two doctors for every one nurse. This creates inefficiencies in service delivery and places fiscal pressure on the budget. Additionally, the inequitable geographic distribution of health workers creates a relative scarcity of high-quality providers in rural areas of the country. Protracted government recruitment procedures and delays exacerbate the situation. The operations at Ministry of Health and Family Welfare (MOHFW) and general government policies and procedures need to be streamlined. The health workers in the government system are not given adequate performance incentives with the result that the quality of health services remains relatively low.

To achieve UHC by 2032 the government will have to pursue a variety of policy reforms to address critical HRH shortages, improve rural retention of health workers, reverse skill-mix distribution ratios between physicians and other cadres of health workers, and improve newborn and maternal health in particular. An important starting point will be streamlining government recruitment and other HRH-related policies. Government processes, including establishing training institutions, developing curricula, and recruiting, transferring, and promoting staff, should be carefully examined. Efforts should be made across government entities to improve these systems.

An overview of the population's health status and use of health care facilities is given in box 1.1, reflecting some of the crucial areas that need to see further progress.

Box 1.1   Good in Parts

In 2011, the infant mortality rate was 43 infant deaths per 1,000 live births, down from 65 in 2004. The simultaneous decline in the death rate for children age 1 to 4 was even greater, from 23 deaths per 1,000 live births to 10. The overall death rate for children age 0 to 4 was 53 per 1,000 live births in 2011. Of children under age 5, 41.3 percent were stunted and 36.4 percent were underweight. Vaccination rates, however, are quite high: the proportion of children receiving all required vaccinations was 86 percent in 2011, including over 90 percent receiving the polio vaccine, with little difference between urban and rural areas (ICF Macro et al. 2012).

In 2011, more than two-thirds of pregnant women received antenatal care (ANC), with 54.6 percent seeking care from a skilled provider. Only 28.8 percent of deliveries took place in a health facility, which is low but still an improvement from a mere 12 percent in 2004. Fewer than half of pregnant women in urban areas gave birth in a health facility, and those in the highest quintile were six times more likely to deliver at a health facility than those in the lowest quintile (ICF Macro et al. 2012). Similarly, only 30.8 percent of pregnant women in the lowest income quintile report receiving antenatal care by a medically trained provider, while 83.6 percent of those in the highest quintile report the same (World Bank 2010). A similar pattern is seen for family planning services (O'Donnell et al. 2007; World Bank 2012).

box continues next page

Box 1.1   Good in Parts *(continued)*

Use of family planning is high at 61.2 percent, including 52.1 percent women who report using modern methods. The contraceptive pill is the most widely used modern method at 27.2 percent, followed by injectables at 11.2 percent, and the male condom at 5.5 percent (ICF Macro et al. 2012).

Utilization of public health services is low: only about 12 percent of deliveries take place at public facilities—the majority are still at home (71 percent). Despite the rise in use of family planning, fewer women report a visit from a government or private family planning worker. Only 15.5 percent of women reported contact with a home visitor, which has been a signifi-cant focus of programmatic activities of MOHFW in recent years. Similarly, only 9 percent of those who sought medical care did so from government facilities, while 14 percent sought care from government doctors in their private practice. Drugstores and pharmacies are vis-ited most often for treatment, with 40 percent of patients reporting visiting them for treat-ment. Treatment from private and nongovernmental organization (NGO) doctors accounted for 25 percent of treatment seeking in 2011 (ICF Macro et al. 2012).

Service delivery system coverage provided by Bangladesh's public health services remains limited due to poor infrastructure and low quality of services. At the upazila level (government health services are delivered by administrative level—appendix A), only 1.2 percent of hospi-tals have 100 percent bed occupancy rates: bed occupancy rate based on actual number of beds was 84.87 percent in the UHCs and only 28.83 percent in Maternal and Child Welfare Centers (MCWCs). About 17 percent of ambulances were not functional at UHC level. Only 27 percent of hospitals had 75 percent of the basic drugs, and only 46 percent of the UHCs reported having at least 75 percent of the basic drugs on the list. Community clinics had 56 percent of the basic drugs, MCWCs 28 percent, and Health and Family Welfare Centers (HFWCs) 11 percent. In the UHCs, out of 34 basic laboratory items, at least 19 items were avail-able in less than 60 percent of the facilities (University of South Carolina [USC] and Associates for Community and Population Research [ACPR] 2012). The nonstate actors and the private, for-profit sector play a key role in providing care, but with uneven quality and little regulation.

All Bangladeshis are technically entitled to receive health care in public health facilities, yet both resources and supply are biased toward urban areas, which create large inequalities in use of services. Even though in aggregate more government resources are dedicated to rural areas, expenditure per capita in rural areas is around half that in urban areas (Ahmed et al. 2005; Bangladesh Health Watch 2012; Werner 2009).

Source: World Bank.

CHAPTER 2

The Path to UHC

The Health Care Financing Strategy

The 2012 Health Care Financing Strategy (Government of Bangladesh 2012a) outlines the roadmap to achieve universal health coverage (UHC) in Bangladesh by 2032. The goal of the strategy is to create one common pool of a universal Social Health Protection Scheme (SHPS). However, Bangladesh will first introduce a noncontributory tax-funded insurance program for the poor (called Shasthyo Suroksha Karmasuchi [SSK]) and a contributory scheme for civil servants, financed through payroll taxes and employers' contributions. The contributory scheme component of the SHPS will be formally known as the formal Social Health Protection Scheme. The informal sector—the remaining share of the population—will rely on community-based health insurance (CBHI) as a first step, and are expected to voluntarily join the national insurance program. In the initial phase, 2012–16, a pilot of SSK was planned for households below the poverty line, but implementation was delayed. It remains, however, a priority program for the government. In the first phase, 2016–21, the Health Protection Fund will be launched, with the intent to cover all households below the poverty line (31.5 percent of the population) through a noncontributory regime, and formal sector households (12.3 percent of population) through a contributory regime (Government of Bangladesh 2012a). During this interim period, community-based health insurance will be promoted for households lacking coverage (56.2 percent of the population). By 2032, the Ministry of Health and Family Welfare (MOHFW) hopes to achieve UHC and integrate all households under the national Health Protection Fund. This plan remains conceptual, with much work needed to make it economically and operationally feasible. Figure 2.1 depicts the proposed evolution of health financing.

The large size of the informal sector—56 percent of the whole population and 87.7 percent of workers—is a critical challenge as the country moves to UHC (Maligalig et al. 2009). Its size suggests it is unlikely that in the next two decades the current plan to rely on micro-health insurance will provide the informal sector adequate coverage. Although CBHI presents opportunities to pool

Figure 2.1   Sequencing of the UHC Plan

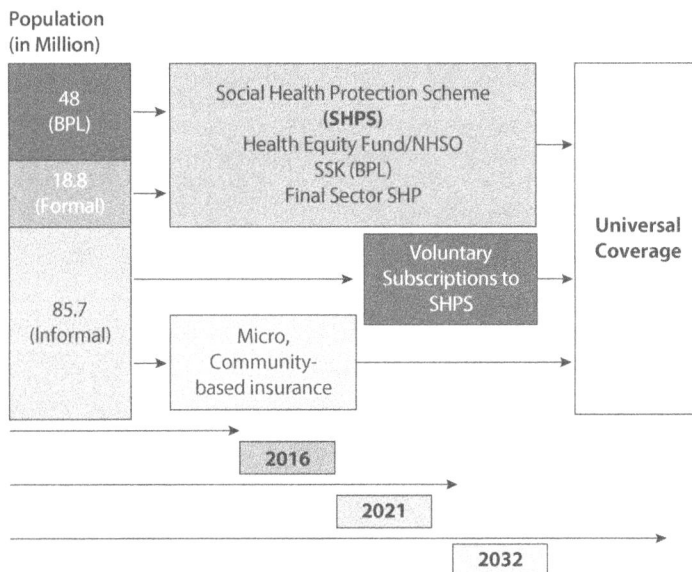

Source: Government of Bangladesh 2012a, p. 17.
Note: BPL = Below poverty line; SHP = Social health protection; SHPS = Social Health Protection Scheme; SSK = Shasthyo Suroksha Karmasuchi; NHSO = National Health Security Office.

resources at the community level and could offer some level of financial protection, estimates show that its ability to effectively protect the population against health costs remains limited in Bangladesh (Bangladesh Health Watch 2012).

The UHC plan expects that out-of-pocket (OOP) spending will decrease from 64 to 32 percent of total health expenditure (THE) once it is fully implemented. Government health spending is planned to increase to cover the decrease in OOP spending, primarily to cover premiums for the poor (figure 2.2).

These plans expect that financing for the scheme will be derived from capturing the current high levels of OOP, and channeling them into prepaid premiums that go directly into the scheme. Even if revenues are effectively collected, it remains unclear how the pooling and redistribution functions of the insurance system will work. The design and implementation of these functions are vital to ensure that the scheme provides financial protection for its beneficiaries. However, it is not expected that OOP spending will substantially decrease over the next two decades because more than half of the population will not be eligible for the scheme until 2032. At the same time, under the UHC plan, government health spending is projected to increase to 30 percent of THE over this interim period. For this to happen though, the government will have to go against WHO estimates that show that government health spending will *decrease* over the next decade as a share of THE (in 2010 it was 34 percent of THE). Without the projected increases in government health spending in the long run, it is unlikely that sufficient resources will be made available to cover the below poverty line (BPL) population's premiums and to make the requisite upgrades to the primary health care system (IMF 2011).

Figure 2.2   Proposed Evolution of Health Financing

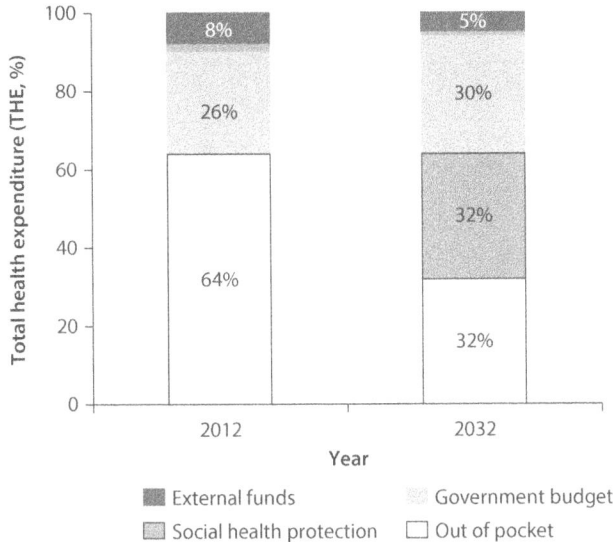

Source: Government of Bangladesh 2012a, p. 11.

If the government plans to cover 40 percent of the UHC plan (its contribution comprising mainly premiums for the BPL population), its budget for health needs to increase annually by 5.4 percent until 2014/15 and 2.0 percent afterwards until 2024/25 (Bangladesh Health Watch 2012). Table 2.1 shows the amount of resources needed to cover the projected costs.

Even so, Bangladesh spends less on health than other countries in South Asia at similar incomes (figure 2.3). While THE nearly tripled in purchasing power parity (PPP) in constant international dollars between 2000 and 2012, Bangladesh continued to spend approximately half of what South Asia spends on health per capita. There are signs that Bangladeshis are placing greater emphasis on health spending with THE as a share of gross domestic product (GDP) increasing from 2.8 percent in 2000 to 3.7 percent in recent years (World Bank 2012).

While the importance of overall spending shows an increasing trend, government health spending as a share of THE has decreased slightly from 38.30 percent on average in 2000–05 to 36.03 percent on average in 2005–10. The budget's share dedicated to health has remained relatively stable at 8.25 percent in 2000–11. Although this is a comparable share to, or even slightly higher than, comparator countries, government revenues to GDP are smaller in Bangladesh than in any other country in the region (16 percent of GDP). In 2011, the tax-to-GDP ratio was 10 percent, indicating limited government capacity to mobilize substantial revenues. Government health spending has been relatively inelastic to the growth of income (averaging 5.9 percent in 2000–12). Official development assistance remains an important source of financing and accounted for 6.6 percent of THE in 2011 (World Bank 2013).

Table 2.1 Public Expenditure Required for UHC

million taka

Indicators	2009/10	2014/15	2019/20	2024/25
A. Population (number)	158,665,000	178,682,560	197,279,985	217,813,044
B. Total public health expenditure ideally required for UHC	274,173	308,763	340,899	376,381
C. Estimated health care budget with 6% growth rate	68,320	91,427	122,350	163,732
D. Deficit to achieve UHC (million taka) (B-C)	205,853	217,335	218,549	212,648
E. Amount of budget if government provides 50% of ideally required budget (50% of B)	137,086	154,382	170,450	188,190
F. Amount of budget if government provides 40% of ideally required budget (40% of B)	109,669	123,505	136,360	150,552
G. Amount of budget if government provides 25% of ideally required budget (25% of B)	68,543	77,190	85,224	94,095

Source: Adapted from Bangladesh Health Watch 2012.
Note: UHC = Universal health coverage.

Figure 2.3 THE Per Capita

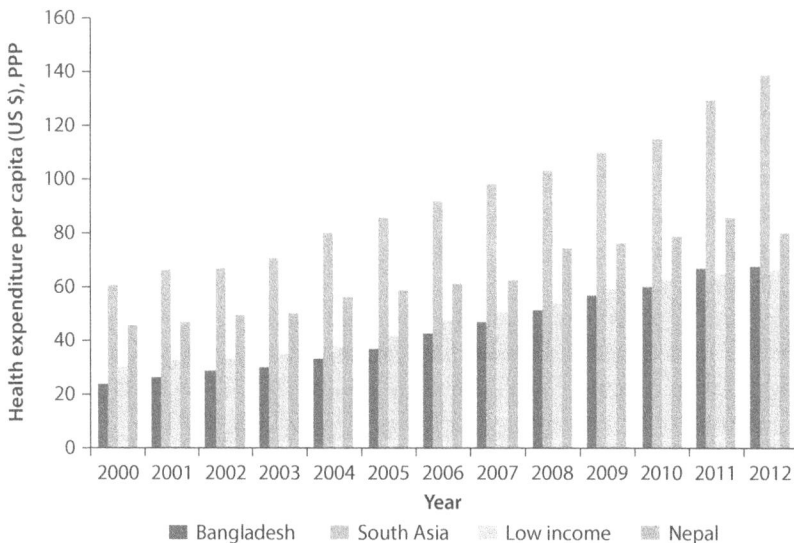

Source: World Development Indicators 2014.
Note: PPP = Purchasing power parity.

As for the health benefits package, Bangladesh has had rapid advancements in coverage of maternal and child health interventions (Chowdhury et al. 2013). However, noncommunicable diseases, treatment of injuries, and high-cost diseases have lagged behind (El-Saharty et al. 2013). The health benefits package may initially expand the coverage for an essential set of highly cost-effective interventions that affect the poor, which may include the treatment of high-cost catastrophic events. These interventions would be publicly financed through a combination of tax revenues and payroll taxes. For the defined benefit package of publicly financed services, there would be no user fees, defined as fee-for-service charges at the point of care.

To achieve UHC, lack of money is not the only constraint. Service delivery is an equally critical component. However, service delivery inefficiencies are compounded by the persistent problems with the health workforce. An effective UHC system also needs health workers of the right type in the right place at the right time with the right skills and in the right working environment. Chapters 3 and 4 provide a detailed analysis of the human resources for health (HRH) training, recruiting, planning, and incentive systems.

CHAPTER 3

HRH

Introduction

The health workforce is a central component in a well-functioning health system. Without adequate numbers of qualified personnel to provide the needed health services, it is not possible to achieve universal health coverage (UHC). The main challenges of human resources for health (HRH) that the government is facing are extreme shortages, low production of nurses, low public sector salaries, delayed recruitment processes, inequitable distribution, skill-mix imbalances, poor-quality/performance of workers, and a nonconducive work environment.[1]

HRH Stock

Bangladesh is experiencing an extreme health workforce crisis. As of 2007, there were only around five physicians and two nurses per 10,000 population (Ahmed et al. 2011), with particular shortages in hard-to-reach areas (Government of Bangladesh 2012a). The same year there were shortages of 91,000 doctors, 273,000 nurses, and 455,000 technologists (Bangladesh Health Watch 2008). The lack of physicians in clinics was one of the four key factors cited by patients who fell ill and chose not to seek care (Ahmed et al. 2006). There were 12 unqualified village doctors and 11 salespeople at drug retail outlets per 10,000 population and twice as many community health workers (CHWs) from nongovernmental organizations (NGOs) than from the government.

Figure 3.1 presents the density of different types of health care providers (HCPs) (Bangladesh Health Watch 2008). Qualified health care professionals (doctors, nurses, dentists) account for 5 percent of the active HCPs.

Even with the growth in training institutions (see below), absolute shortages of health workers will continue in the coming years. In addition to shortages of skilled health workers, numbers of public health professionals and managers, who are needed to assist in the UHC planning and implementation process, are

Figure 3.1 Density of HCPs per 10,000 Population

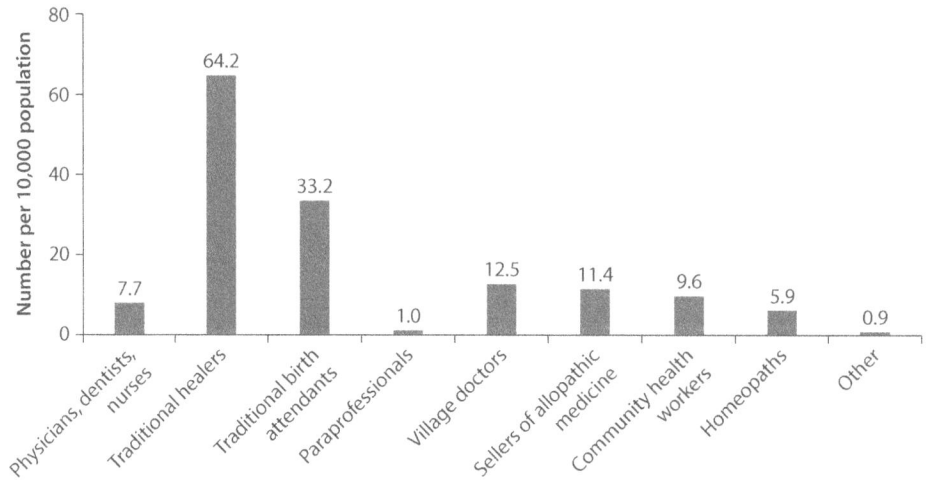

Source: Bangladesh Health Watch 2008, p. 7 (figure 2.1).

also inadequate. There would appear to be shortages across all categories, but in case of anesthetists and nurses the shortage is acute. Shortages stem from inadequate HRH production combined with migration and other trends (box 3.1), an inordinately slow recruitment process, and difficulty in staff retention particularly in remote areas (discussed below).

Some leakage from the HRH stock also occurs as dropouts from the profession. The recent trend of feminization of the health workforce had a positive effect in bringing about changes in communities through the massive and unprecedented deployment of diverse cadres of mostly female frontline health workers to bring high-priority services to every household in the country (Mushtaque et al. 2013). However, many female physicians, nurses, medical technologists, or paraprofessionals choose to remain as housewives after marriage and become inactive in their profession, and this may occur for a limited time or for the long term. It also becomes difficult to post them in remote rural and hard-to-reach areas due to lack of infrastructure and other sociocultural reasons. Similarly, many health professionals choose to leave the health sector. Many trained HRH pursue a business. Some physicians become civil servants, for instance, in the magistracy, foreign service, and police.

These shortages persist despite consistent increases in the workforce (figure 3.2). As of 2013, out of 64,434 registered doctors, only 46,951 were available in the country. Of these, 38 percent worked in the public sector, the rest in the private sector. Similarly, the estimated number of registered nurses in the country was 30,516, of whom only 13,235 (43 percent) were in the public sector (DGHS 2014).

Box 3.1 The Brain Drain and Other Lost Assets

The shortage of qualified doctors in the country is compounded by the fact that the "brain drain" (migration of skilled workforce abroad) is relentless. According to an estimate, there were 1,794 registered Bangladeshi doctors working in the United States, Canada, United Kingdom, Australia, New Zealand, and Saudi Arabia until March 2001 (Peters and Kayne 2003). This is a gross underestimate because data are not available for other Middle Eastern countries and India, and no current data are available. It is estimated that on an average, 200 doctors from the government sector go abroad every year (Adkoli 2006). Besides, medical technologists and some nurses also migrate annually, but no reliable data are available.

A major constraint is the ineffectiveness of medical education and training programs in Bangladesh. A survey of 132 medical students found that the majority wanted to specialize in established clinical specialties and practice in major cities. Half of all respondents intended to try to migrate abroad to practice (Ahmed, Majumdar et al. 2011). This finding is not surprising, given the result of Jenkins et al. (2010) that Bangladesh would have twice the number of psychiatrists per 100,000 population without migration abroad.

Source: World Bank.

Figure 3.2 Health Workforce Registered with the Bangladesh Medical and Dental Council (BMDC) and Bangladesh Nursing Council (BNC), 1997, 2007, and 2013

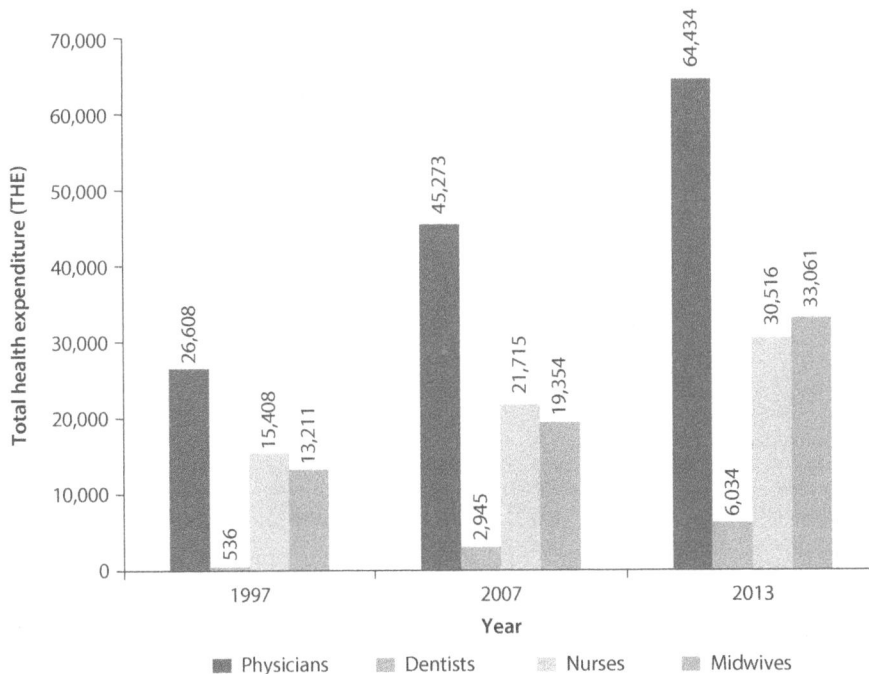

Source: DGHS 1997, 2007, and 2014, and United Nations Population Fund (UNFPA) 2011.
Note: Midwives are in fact nurses with midwifery competencies (UNFPA 2011).

HRH Production

Annual production capacity of health workers is shown table 3.1. While the number of institutes and places ("seats") have been increasing recently, the trend of production is unlikely to fulfill the gaps whether in numbers or health needs. For example, the total number of seats for doctors continues to be more than double those for nurses,[2] thus perpetuating the reversed doctor-to-nurse ratio. Apart from BSc nursing, there are more seats for admission for doctors, diploma nurses, medical technologists, and medical assistants in the private sector than in the public sector. These cadres cater mainly to the needs of the private sector as they are highly likely to work in curative health services and mostly in urban areas and will not cover the acute shortages in primary health care services in rural areas. There has also been a relatively large increase in the number of unqualified allopathic providers during the past decade, as compared to qualified or semiqualified allopathic providers. This huge proliferation of unqualified health workers is indicative of the weak regulatory bodies despite repeated policy commitments to strengthen them. Despite multiple initiatives in the last decade, there still remain significant weaknesses in medical education. For example, implementation of a new undergraduate medical curriculum is still partial,

Table 3.1 Annual Production Capacity of Health Workforce Including Private Sector, 2011

A. HRH categories	Number of institutes			Number of seats for admission		
	Total	Public	Private	Total	Public	Private
Physicians						
Postgraduate	32	22	10	2,237	2,068	169
Medical college	77	23	54	7,285	3,010	4,275
Dental college	23	9	14	1,428	578	850
Subtotal for physicians	**143**	**54**	**78**	**10,474**	**5,180**	**5,294**
Medical assistants	92	8	84	5,705	700	5,005
Nurses and allied HRH						
Nursing (Diploma)	82	43	39	2,390	870	1,520
Nursing (BSc)	30	13	17	1,775	1,275	500
Midwifery	11	n.a.	11	300	n.a.	300
Community skilled birth attendant	47	45	2	n.a.	n.a.	n.a.
Specialized nursing	4	n.a.	4	80	n.a.	80
Subtotal for nurses and allied HRH	**174**	**101**	**73**	**4,545**	**2,145**	**2,400**
Medical technologists						
Inst. of health technology (Diploma)	82	7	75	10,657	2,041	8,616
Inst. of health technology (BSc)	22	3	19	1,715	265	1,450
Subtotal for medical technologists	**104**	**10**	**94**	**12,372**	**2,306**	**10,066**

Source: World Bank calculation from Bangladesh Health Bulletin 2012.
Note: HRH = Human resources for health; n.a. = Not applicable.

Box 3.2 Training Innovations

A partnership program with Canadian volunteers to train Bangladeshi nurses was effective in improving education for these nurses (Berland et al. 2010). Some nongovernmental organizations (NGOs) adapted a group-based national family planning in-service training curriculum to an on-the-job training program, so as to avoid taking health workers away from their posts (Murphy 2008). Another attempt to improve the skills capacity of medical staff in Bangladesh found that health workers had the time to take up additional activities for active visceral leishmaniasis (black fever) case detection as part of their day-to-day workload (Naznin et al. 2013).

Source: World Bank.

undergraduate training of medical students in rural settings faces obstacles, and there are no plans in place to implement a postgraduate training program. Still, some innovative training programs have shown promise (box 3.2).

Public Sector Salaries

Public salaries in health follow national pay scale for government employees. The entry-level salary scale (table 3.2) is very modest, and is inadequate for most of the health workers to sustain themselves at a decent level. Similar data are available for the private sector. However, for comparison, a fresh medical graduate gets anywhere between Tk 20,000 to 30,000, depending upon location of workplace or nature of the organization (national, UN bodies, and international NGOs have different salary structures).

Vacancy Rates and Recruitment

Of the sanctioned[3] public posts for doctors, 27 percent remain unfilled; more widely, 20 percent of the 115,530 posts under the Directorate General of Health Services (DGHS) are vacant (DGHS 2012)—and some have been vacant for years (figure 3.3).

The vacancy litany continues: 21 percent of posts for medical technologists (pharmacy, laboratory, radiography, radiotherapy, physiotherapy, dental); 9 percent for midlevel resources (Sub-assistant Community Medical Officer [SACMO], domiciliary staff including assistant health inspector and health assistants); and 13.4 percent in nursing services.

This high number of vacancies stems from several factors. First, the entire process—from identification of a vacancy to final hiring—can take up to three years in the public sector, partly because several government bodies are involved. Thus, if Ministry of Health and Family Welfare (MOHFW) requisitions the Public Service Commission (PSC) for physicians due to vacancies, the PSC

Table 3.2 Basic Pay Scale for Different Cadres of Health Professionals under Public Sector

Grade	Basic pay scale (effective July 1, 2009)
9 (Doctor)	Tk 11,000–490×7–14,430–EBᵃ–540× 11–20,370
10 (Nurse)	Tk 8,000–450×7–11,150–EB–490×11–16,540
11 (Medical assistant)	Tk 6,400–415×7–9,305–EB–450×11–13,125
14 (Family welfare visitor)	Tk 5,200–320×7–7,440–EB–345×11–11,235
16 (Health assistant/family welfare assistant)	Tk 4,700–265×7–6,555–EB–290×11–9,745

Source: Government of Bangladesh 2009a.
Note: Salary excludes house rent, medical allowance, conveyance allowance, festival bonus, and so on, which add about 50–60 percent to the basic salary.
a. EB = Estimated benefit.

Figure 3.3 Filled-In Posts as Percentage of Sanctioned Posts by Year

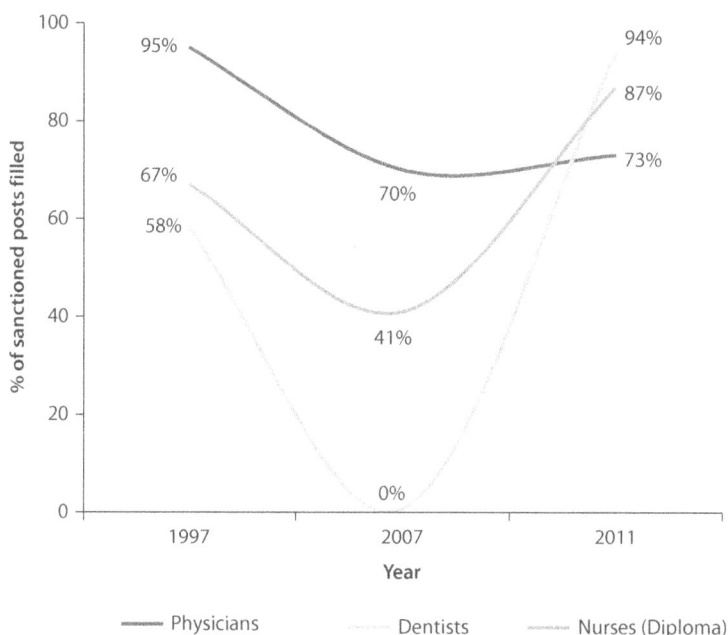

Source: Ahmed and Sabur 2013.

manages to supply them only after two or three years (figure 3.4), by which time MOHFW already incurs similar vacancies due to staff turnover and retirement as well as expansion of health service facilities.[4] The long PSC exam procedure and slow notification to the MOHFW of the approved vacant posts are among the key factors in this delay.

The problem of unfilled posts is compounded by staff absenteeism, mainly of doctors and nurses, which may range from 7.5 to 40.0 percent on any particular day (Chaudhury and Hammer 2004;University of South Carolina [USC] and Associates for Community and Population Research [ACPR] 2012).

There is a serious information gap about the number of active health personnel. Professional councils produce cumulative data that are not useful for

Figure 3.4 Process and Responsibilities for Creation of a New Post

National Implementation Committee for Adminstrative Reforms — Final Approval for creation of new post — Need identified and determined — *MoHFW*

Justification approved for new post — *Ministry of Establishment*

Funding of new post approved — *Ministry of Finance*

Committee of Secretaries — Preparation for submission to Cabinet

Cabinet Ministry — Cabinet Approval to create new post

Source: World Bank 2010, p. 83.

planning processes. Health workers assigned to posts have to take on the extra work that should be handled by the vacant posts. As a result of this extra burden, the quality of their services inevitably declines.

Because health workers in the public sector are part of the civil service, recruitment and deployment, along with career progression and incentives, are all governed by civil service regulations, which are outside the purview of the MOHFW. Hence, the MOHFW has little control over these processes and any reforms have to be governmentwide civil service reform—which is inevitably slow.

The PSC is entrusted with recruiting classes I and II employees.[5] And although the local authority (like the head of hospitals or the civil surgeon) is authorized to recruit classes III and IV employees, they need to seek permission from DGHS, which cuts down 20 percent of the requisition almost routinely.

The hard-to-reach areas have far worse vacancy rates than the national figures discussed above, as most workers want to live and work in major urban metropolitan areas (giving them fewer vacancies)—one of the major factors in the inequitable distribution of health staff in Bangladesh.

HRH Distribution—Facts and Factors

Ten Times Better in Towns

The heavy urban bias in the health workforce has been a persistent issue in Bangladesh for decades (Ahmed, Hossain et al. 2011). Most qualified personnel concentrate in major cities—disproportionately in Dhaka Division (out of seven divisions) including Dhaka City, since almost all specialized and teaching hospitals are in Dhaka City (figure 3.5)—while hard-to-reach areas are left with unqualified or semiqualified personnel. Of the national population, 15 percent (in Dhaka, Chittagong, Rajshahi, and Khulna) are served by 35 percent of physicians and 30 percent of nurses. Fewer than 20 percent of the HRH are providing services to more than 75 percent of the rural population. The doctor-to-population ratio is 1:1,500 in urban areas and 10 times worse in rural areas—1:15,000 (Mabud 2005).

The urban–rural maldistribution has existed in Bangladesh for decades, and successive governments have not been entirely successful in resolving this challenge. For example, the focus of the first five-year plan (1973–78) was to establish health complexes at rural level (in Bengali, upazila) and offer minimal health services as close to the community as resources permitted. Efforts were made by successive governments to ensure availability of qualified HRH in these areas on a regular basis, but these efforts proved unsuccessful. The translation of policies into practice has always been hindered by political interference in areas such as establishing HRH educational institutions outside the major cities, compulsory

Figure 3.5   Rural–Urban Distribution of HCPs by Type

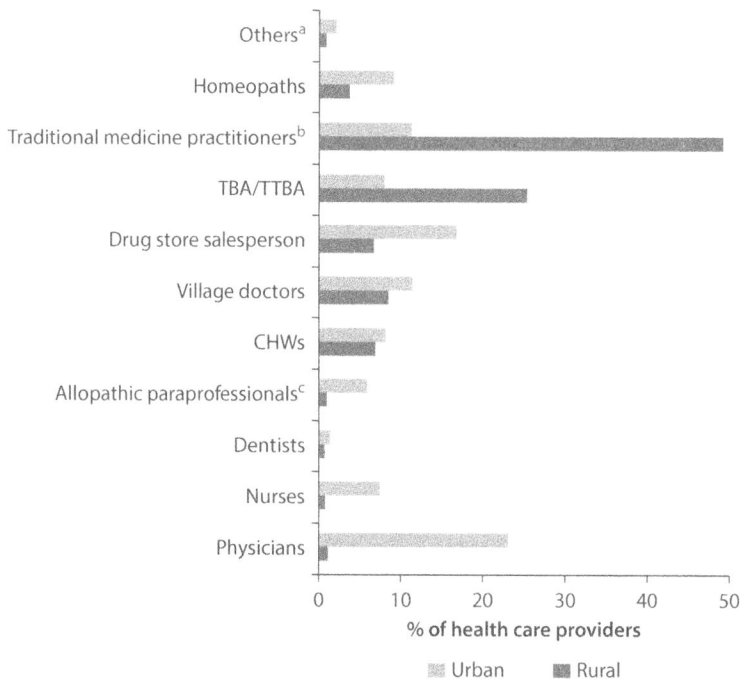

Source: Bangladesh Health Watch 2008, p. 8 (table 2.1).
Note: TBA = Traditional birth attendant; TTBA = Trained Traditional Birth Attendant;
CHWs = Community health workers.
a. Circumcision practitioners, tooth extractors, ear cleaners etc.
b. Herbalists, faith-healers.
c. Medical assistants/Sub-assistant Community Medical Officers, Family welfare visitors, and lab technicians/physiotherapists.

service in rural areas, or structuring a career ladder (Joarder, Uddin, and Islam 2013). Rigid civil service rules and weak implementation capacity have been factors that hinder progress toward improving the distribution of health workers.

Despite the commitments of the Health and Population Sector Program (HPSP [1998-2003]) and National Health Policy (NHP 2000[6]) to avoid imbalances in the distribution of human resources, deep geographic imbalances remain, partly because the underlying factors have not been resolved (box 3.3). There are, for example, no incentives for posting and retaining health workers in remote and hard-to-reach areas (Government of Bangladesh 2008).

The 2008 HR Policy on Transfer and Posting for officers in health service offers two years of rural posting as an incentive for better career for the doctors. But, in practice, this commitment has not removed doctors' fear of being "stuck" in rural areas. Many medical staff, therefore, avoid remote postings or take the posting but arrange secondments to higher-level facilities in city areas, leaving their posts officially filled but effectively vacant.

Box 3.3   Push and Pull Factors—All toward Urban Areas

Most doctors posted to rural areas do not remain there, as they prefer to do private practice in big cities. Both pull and push factors are at work. Concentration of higher-level facilities in the urban areas, prospects of good private practice, opportunities for higher education and training, standard of living, and lifestyle, all pull the professionals (especially doctors) out of the rural areas. Similarly, there are also factors such as lack of adequate infrastructure, supporting staff, and supplies in rural facilities; political interference; lack of clear rules for "reward and punishment"; absence of rules for rural postings and subsequent promotion and education opportunities; standard of living and lifestyle, which all push professionals (especially doctors) toward urban areas.

As most educational and training institutions are in urban/peri-urban areas, students/ trainees spend considerable time in these areas and thus get accustomed to the urban lifestyle and facilities. These may be difficult to sacrifice when entering professional life. Though a prerequisite for admission into postgraduate courses for physicians is two years of rural service (reduced to one year for basic sciences), admissions into postgraduate courses are competitive, and those residing in urban centers enjoy more facilities for preparation, which can also pull physicians out of rural areas. The National Health Policy 2011 proposed to increase the duration of internship for medical graduates from one year to two years and post the intern for one year in the rural facilities so that the current crisis can be met to some extent (Government of Bangladesh 2012b).

There are no posts for the nurses below the upazila health complex (UZHC) level, due to the physicians' perception that nurses are not good enough to be left unsupervised. This notion might have stemmed from the country's sociocultural norm of demeaning the nursing profession (Hadley et al. 2007), which eventually hindered nurse deployment in rural areas.

Source: World Bank.

Figure 3.6   Distribution of HCPs by Divisions (per 10,000 population)

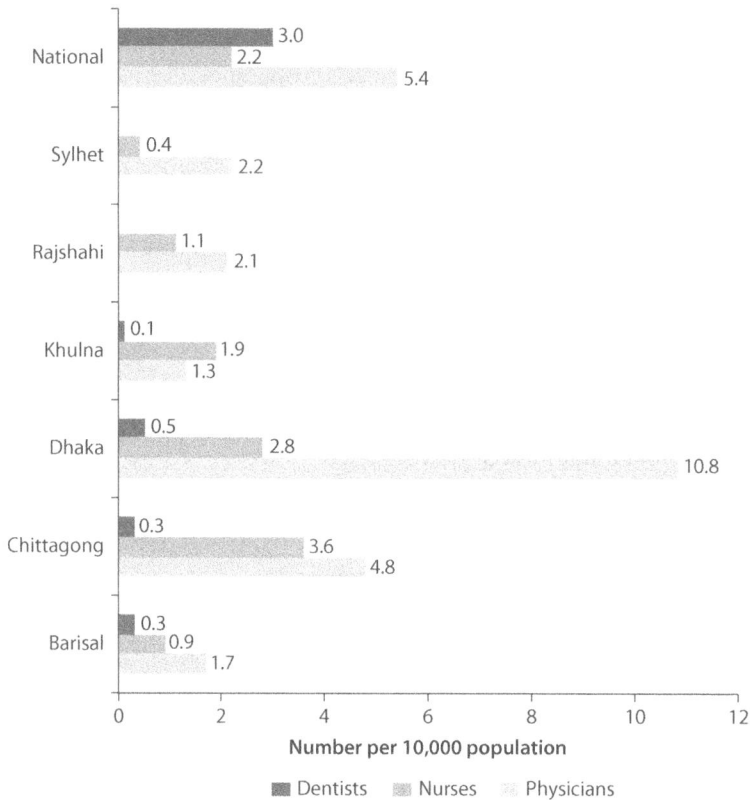

Source: Bangladesh Health Watch 2008, p. 9 (table 2.2).

The workforce distribution of all health workers massively favors Dhaka and other metropolitan areas (figure 3.6). The largest number of posts of doctors are sanctioned for Dhaka Division (8,203), followed by Chittagong (3,745), with the lowest for Sylhet (1,460) (DGHS 2012). On the other hand, the rate of vacant posts for doctors is the lowest in Dhaka (17 percent of the sanctioned post), while in other divisions the average vacancy rate is 33 percent. Only in Khulna division does the proportion of nurses per 10,000 population exceed that of the doctors.

The private sector workforce also shares the unequal urban–rural split. Dhaka has more private doctors than other metropolitan districts. Unequal distribution affects service provision through a scarcity of providers.

Gender Imbalances

Geography is not the only imbalance. There are higher vacancy rates and lower numbers of female health workers in rural areas, which deteriorates the situation to an even greater extent. Though HPSP (1998–2003) and NHP 2000 and the policies and programs onwards advocated for women-friendly health service delivery, in practice, policy commitment has not been reflected in the staffing pattern. Gender imbalance continues to exist in the staffing pattern. The majority of doctors, dentists, technicians, and pharmacists are male, while the majority of nurses are female. In family planning services, most providers are women and almost all supervisors are men. Policy-making, management, and training positions are mostly occupied by male employees—a situation that causes underrepresentation of the needs specific to women.

Conversely, unqualified/semiqualified allopathic practitioners such as the village doctors and CHWs are concentrated in rural areas, while drugstore attendants are a little more evenly distributed between the two types of areas (see figure 3.5). There is also the usual stock of traditional healers and traditional birth attendants—primarily in rural areas—who account for the vast majority of HCPs (box 3.4).

Box 3.4 Informal Sector/Semiqualified and Allopathic Providers

In 2007, informal sector providers constituted 88 percent of HCPs (Ahmed, Hossain and Chowdhury 2009). In a study of health care utilization patterns in a remote area of Bangladesh, Mahmood et al. (2010) found that of the 47 percent of ill people who sought care, some 65 percent consulted the village doctor.

The continued reliance on these informal and traditional practitioners (especially in rural areas) has led to several studies promoting the integration of these providers with the formal system, partly to overcome shortages among maternal health providers and to treat elderly patients (most of whom are used to seeking care outside the formal health system) (Hossen 2010; Mollik et al. 2009; Mridha, Anwar, and Koblinsky 2009).

Two studies however found that traditional practitioners can be integrated into the formal health system to provide targeted outreach, diagnostic, and treatment services. Through training, traditional village doctors could refer tuberculosis (TB) cases with positive sputum smears (11 percent of all cases) and administer a directly observed treatment short-course (DOTS) (20–45 percent of patients between 1998 and 2003) (Hamid et al. 2006). Nonformal providers provided sexually transmitted infection (STI) counseling consistent with national guidelines after private pharmaceutical companies disseminated targeted information on these guidelines. Specifically, 44 percent of mystery clients in intervention areas received STI counseling from nonformal providers as compared to 0 percent in control areas (Sarma and Oliveras 2011).

Yet, a study of unqualified providers (drugstore sales people and village doctors) and semiqualified workers found that these groups generally lacked the appropriate training and ability to provide basic services (Ahmed and Hossain 2007). The informal sector providers' main routes of entry into the profession are apprenticeship and inheritance and/or short training of few weeks to a few months duration from semiformal, unregulated private institutions. As such, their professional knowledge base is not at a level necessary for providing basic curative services with minimum acceptable quality of care (Ahmed and Hossain 2007; Ahmed, Hossain, and Chowdhury 2009).

---

box continues next page

However, the CHWs trained by NGOs fared better than the unqualified providers in terms of rational use of drugs for common illness and the management of pregnancy and reproductive health-related interventions. NGOs generally were good at improving the skills and knowledge of CHWs. Further, CHWs trained by formal institutions of the government or NGOs were better than other informal allopathic providers (for example, village doctors and salespeople at drug retail outlets) in providing some specific services such as DOTS for tuberculosis (Chowdhury et al. 1997) and acute respiratory infections of children (Hadi 2003), including rational use of drugs (Ahmed and Hossain 2007). Their services have also been found to be cost-effective (Islam et al. 2002). The role of CHWs is discussed further in box 3.5.

Source: World Bank.
Note: See appendix C for more details.

Box 3.5 Community Health Workers

Community health workers have been a cornerstone of Bangladesh's health workforce since the 1970s, when the government began using female CHWs to assist in home deliveries. Due to absolute health workforce shortages, CHWs are a low-cost way to provide basic outreach and health services. CHWs take on a wide range of tasks, including assisting deliveries, providing basic diagnostic services for sick children, and promoting modern contraception. Due to the short duration of training needed and low input costs, various studies and pilots have introduced interventions to train or introduce CHWs to provide a variety of services in Bangladesh.

CHWs have been found to be a highly cost-effective way to deliver certain basic health services in Bangladesh. For instance, Islam et al. (2002) found that the use of Bangladesh Rural Advancement Committee (BRAC) CHWs in providing TB services cost $64 per patient cured, as compared to $96 if those services were provided by government workers. In rural areas, the BRAC CHW program could cure three TB patients for every two in the government program areas.

This level of effectiveness extends to the promotion of contraceptive practices. Household survey data from 2004 found that home visits by female CHWs were a strong predictor of modern contraceptive use, even after controlling for other covariates (Kamal and Mohsena 2007).

Home visits by CHWs can also play an important role in infant and child health. Home visits by CHWs within two days following birth reduced neonatal mortality by 67 percent (Baqui et al. 2009). This positive impact on neonatal survival may be even greater if the home visits are combined with participatory women's groups. CHWs were also able to accurately identify severe acute malnutrition among children (Puett et al. 2012). Specifically, a study of CHWs' management of severe acute malnutrition found the majority were able to effectively use a quality of care checklist (89.1 percent) and achieved a 90 percent error-free case management (Puett et al. 2013). With targeted training, lower-level and volunteer workers were able to ensure that 87 percent of all neonates in the intervention area received a proper cord-care regimen (Shah et al. 2010).

box continues next page

Box 3.5   Community Health Workers *(continued)*

These findings are aligned with those of Baqui et al. (2009) that found that CHWs trained to identify the signs and symptoms of newborn illness by using a clinical algorithm in rural Bangladesh were highly effective in completing their task. They were able to correctly classify very severe disease in newborns with a sensitivity of 91 percent and specificity of 95 percent. Furthermore, they were able to diagnose almost all signs and symptoms of newborn illness with more than 60 percent sensitivity and 97 to 100 percent specificity. CHWs trained to screen young children in rural Bangladesh for hearing impairments were also effective in compensating for a shortage of trained audiologists (Berg et al. 2006). In addition to diagnosis, CHWs have been found to be effective in increasing self-referral of sick newborns for care (Bari et al. 2006).

The majority of studies on the experience of using CHWs for basic outreach and health services in Bangladesh come to positive conclusions. Standing and Chowdhury (2008) stress that careful selection, training, and supervision by local agents for legitimacy, financial incentives that are sustainable, and integration of CHWs in the formal sector are all important factors in determining the success of such interventions.

Yet, CHW dropout rates are high. Rahman et al. (2010) found the most common factors for these were dissatisfaction with pay, heavy workload, night visits, working outside of one's home area, and familial opposition. Financial incentives have been found to be the most effective in motivating CHW performance and reducing dropout rates in their jobs. However, nonfinancial incentives, such as social prestige, positive community feedback, feeling needed by the community, and potential for career advancement, were also positively associated with willingness to take on a greater workload level (Alam et al. 2012a, 2012b; Rahman et al. 2010).

Source: World Bank.

Skill-mix Imbalances

Since independence, the health sector has emphasized the development of heath infrastructure, as well as the expansion of HRH. However, the focus was aligned with the production of doctors, which has resulted in a serious shortage of support staff, particularly nurses. Although the density (per 10,000 population) of physicians and nurses had increased over the previous decade (from 1.9 physicians and 1.1 nurses in 1998 to 5.4 physicians and 2.1 nurses in 2007) (World Bank 2010), it remained much lower than the estimated average for low-income countries in 1998 (Hossain and Begum 1998). The density of dentists also increased, but remains very low (from 0.01 in 1998 to 0.30 in 2007).

In 2011, doctors made up 70 percent of the total registered professional workforce, and the remaining 30 percent are support staff (Government of Bangladesh 2012a). There are 2.5 times more doctors than nurses in the country (Ahmed, Hossain et al. 2011). With a ratio of 0.4 nurses to 1 doctor, Bangladesh falls far short of the World Health Organization (WHO)-recommended standard of 3 nurses for 1 physician; in fact the ratio is inverted, at 0.4:1.0.

Also among doctors, specialist doctors represent less than a quarter of all doctors; and internal medicine, surgery, gynecology and obstetrics, and, to a lesser extent, pediatrics are better represented, forming around 60 percent of those with a degree in clinical or basic disciplines (Begum 1997). Disciplines such as urology, dermatology, gastroenterology, nephrology, and mental health are almost not represented.

HPSP (1998–2003) recommended increasing the required number and mix of personnel; this has not been implemented. The number of nurses, paramedics, pharmacists, and dentists is too low compared to the number of doctors. The current Health, Population, and Nutrition Sector Development Program includes planned increases in doctors from 5,000 to 6,000 between 2011 and 2016, and planned increases in nurses from 2,700 to 4,000 over the same time period (MOHFW 2012), which would not address these imbalances. In August 2014, Prime Minister Sheikh Hasina announced that 10,000 more nurses would be appointed in the public sector hospitals and clinics and that an institution for postgraduate nursing studies would also be established.

The inappropriate skill-mix of the workforce inhibits a smooth functioning of teamwork. Particularly in the current context of primary health care provision through essential services package from one-stop centers, inappropriate skill-mix is a great barrier to effective service delivery.

HRH Quality and Productivity

Quality of health care provision is mixed but mostly poor. The perceived performance of nurses and doctors is an important determinant of patient satisfaction and utilization of hospitals in Bangladesh (Andaleeb et al. 2007; Andaleeb 2008). A survey used to assess the quality of health service delivery for sick children found that the behavior of nurses and doctors was highly impactful on reported patient satisfaction. In particular, facilitation payments made to health workers were viewed negatively. The poor ratings of both types of health workers by patients highlights the need for additional behavior and technical training to ensure patients seek care when needed (Andaleeb 2008). These results mirror those by Andaleeb et al. (2007), who found that doctors' service orientation was the most important factor explaining patient satisfaction in public and private hospitals in Dhaka. Poor quality was cited as a pervasive problem in a study of care provided to sick children aged under five years in first-level government health facilities. In particular, few of the children were fully assessed or correctly treated and caregivers were not advised on how to continue the care of the child at home. Cases where care was managed by lower-level health workers were significantly more likely to be classified correctly, and caregivers were provided proper instructions for home care. The authors concluded that quality of care needs to be improved in these facilities and that targeting training at lower-level workers may be beneficial.

Apart from the Bangladesh Medical and Dental Council registration requirements, there is no systematic process to assess quality of physician care in Bangladesh, whether in public or private sectors. Findings from a few small-scale studies indicate that there is significant room to improve the technical quality of care provided by them (Arifeen et al. 2005; Chowdhury, Hossain, and Halim 2009; Hasan 2012). The majority of studies examining the performance of the health workforce in Bangladesh target what is not working and highlight potential areas of focus for training activities—revealing significant gaps in assessing performance of health care providers.

Productivity of HCPs is low. Studies show that nurses in Bangladesh spend only a tiny fraction of their duty times on patient care, sometimes as low as 5 percent in government hospitals (Hadley et al. 2007; Zaman 2009). The main reasons behind this low productivity are societal norms related to stigmatization and low status of the profession, which cause nurses in government hospitals to try and distance themselves from patients. Also, because of nurse shortages, the ones working are overextended and unable to provide adequate care for patients. On the other hand, nurses in NGO hospitals seemed to have more direct contact with patients. Discrimination also came through in a study that found a high level of discriminatory attitudes about human immunodeficiency virus/acquired immune deficiency syndrome (HIV/AIDS) among 526 health care workers in Bangladesh (Hossain and Kippax 2010).

Work Environment

The shortage of health workers leads to excess workload for those currently employed in both private and public sectors. Apart from the workload, factors that undermine health workers' morale and contribute to a negative work environment include inadequate supply of drugs and equipment, weak administrative support, lack of scope for career progression, limited in-service training opportunities, and restrictive civil service incentive structures. Excessive workload coupled with negative work environment leads to skilled health workers leaving the profession or migrating to other countries.

Health infrastructure and supplies are inadequate. Some of the problems of poor performance of doctors and nurses in Bangladesh may also be due to health system and infrastructure constraints. For instance, a survey of health workers showed that 45 percent reported difficulties in fulfilling their assigned duties (Cockcroft, Milne, and Andersson 2004). Respondents cited inadequate supplies and infrastructure, bad behavior of patients, and administrative problems as contributing factors to their inability to fulfill their patient responsibilities.

Dual-job holding is exacerbating the problem. Private practice by doctors employed in government jobs (termed "dual practice"), sometimes at the cost of access and quality for the patients, is a common problem in low- and middle-income countries, especially South and Southeast Asia (Hipgraved, Nachtnebel, and Hort 2013), and Bangladesh is no exception. Other than the residency training posts, there is no provision of reasonable nonpracticing allowances for institutional practice that discourages physicians from private practice and focuses them instead on the primary job (Government of Bangladesh 2008). Thus, due to the lack of appropriate incentives in government health services, and to the poor regulation of their activities, doctors tend to compensate low salaries by earning from dual practice. Dual practice becomes especially prevalent when there is a thriving private sector.

Career mobility of health workers is limited. The existing career development plan for doctors is not well designed. Although seniority and merit should be the criteria for promotion, no standard rule is in place for the promotion of doctors. Transfer and posting policy for doctors are another gray area as no clear guideline exists for transfer/posting for any categories of personnel. Political affiliation to the party in power often plays a critical role in rewarding promotion and postings, which significantly demotivates government health workers.

Nurses also have a highly discouraging career plan. Nursing positions are not comparable with the regular hierarchy of health services. The Director (Nursing) is considered equivalent to the Deputy Director, Health Services. The Directorate of Nursing Services and Bangladesh Nursing Council are two key bodies managing nursing education and services. No regular director of nursing was posted since 1993 in the Directorate of Nursing Services (Government of Bangladesh 2011). Job descriptions for nurses are quite old and have been neither reviewed nor updated in recent years. However, efforts are being made to increase the stature of nurses by upgrading their civil service classification from class III to class II.

Notes

1. Appendix A presents a brief description of the health service delivery system, including staffing at primary health centers (PHCs) and HRH production.

2. Until recently, nurses were class III employees—the same level as drivers with a grade 8 education. This may have been another reason why the profession did not attract candidates with higher aptitude to enroll in nursing education.

3. Sanctioned positions are those that are approved and budgeted.

4. The key players are shown in figure 4.1.

5. In the civil service, all employees are categorized into four classes—I, II, III, and IV. Physicians are class I, nurses class II (previously class III), and the rest (medical technologists, paraprofessionals, field workers, and so on) class III employees. This "upgrading" (or some would say, "recognition") of the role of nurses attests to official concern over the lack of nurses in the country.

6. The NHP 2000 committed to deploying one doctor in each Union Health and Family Welfare Centre with all residential facilities but has failed to achieve this.

CHAPTER 4

HRH Policy-Making Process

Introduction

To begin to address the human resources for health (HRH) challenges described in chapter 3, the government of Bangladesh and Ministry of Health and Family Welfare (MOHFW) will need to start with its policy-making processes and procedures. These systems currently impair progress toward meeting stated commitments to improve the country's health workforce in the numerous policy documents and plans that are put out by the government of Bangladesh. The government of Bangladesh will need to reform its processes and invest in implementation capacity in order to begin to address the necessary changes to reach universal health coverage (UHC) with a skilled health workforce in place.

Major HRH Challenges

Despite the government's efforts to introduce reforms to expand and improve the health workforce, many challenges remain. These can be attributed partly to the HRH policy-making environment, which is characterized by the following factors, among others:

- A complex and sometimes contradictory array of national policies with a history of mixed results
- A highly centralized and cumbersome bureaucratic system with weak response capacity that has stifled innovation and at times fueled corruption
- A range of powerful stakeholders, some with competing interests.
- A weak regulatory and enforcement capacity, contributing to high rates of absenteeism and many unqualified health workers

Bangladesh, with the support of international donors, has tried to develop a health policy that recognizes and addresses the human resource challenges in the health sector. Yet, the MOHFW has been unable to design policies or fully implement proposed plans for health workforce improvements. As the government attempts to follow through with Prime Minister Sheikh Hasina's declaration to achieve UHC for all citizens of Bangladesh at the 64th World Health Assembly in May 2011, it will have to overcome what has hindered or blocked implementation of previous HRH-related policies.

The government also needs to invest resources to improve coordination and managerial capacity within government entities involved in designing and implementing policies. This chapter discusses the challenges associated with implementing these plans, as well as other constraining policy-making factors.

A Complex and Sometimes Contradictory Array of National Policies

As the government works to expand and improve its health workforce to implement its plans to achieve UHC by 2032, it should also carefully assess the successes and failures of previous efforts to reform the country's health workforce. Beginning in the early 1970s, with the support of international donors the government has tried to address problems with its health workforce through a series of health sector plans and projects. Before 2000, targets, goals, and strategies for the overall health sector were incorporated into the government's national Five-Year Plans.[1] The country is currently under its sixth Five-Year Plan (2011–15).

The Five-Year Plans lay out the government's broad policy objectives for all sectors, one of which is health. However, they do not provide details on how the health sector plans to allocate resources and introduce policies and programs to then reach these objectives. Alongside these Five-Year Plans were five-year operational projects, primarily funded by the World Bank and other bilateral donors that gave strategic directions specifically for the health sector. These operational projects intended to provide donor financing and strategic direction to implement the policy objectives included in the broader Five-Year Plans. These projects, which began in 1976, were transformed under the Fifth Project into a wider health program called the Health and Population Sector Program (1998–2003). Since then there have been two follow-on programs: the Health, Nutrition, and Population Sector Program (2003–11) and the Health, Nutrition, and Population Sector Development Program (2011–16), which have served as the primary vehicles for HRH policy development and program support.

In addition to these broader health policies and programs, HRH policy has been developed through donor-led health and population projects and National Health Workforce Strategies. These are all under the auspices of the MOHFW and therefore contain overlapping agendas, but are not necessarily coordinated.

Table 4.1 presents the numerous plans and programs in HRH policy since the early 1970s. As global health sector development trends have shifted, so too has the policy focus of these HRH-related components. For instance, in the 1970s and 1980s, a greater focus was placed on primary care and rural health care initiatives in response to the Alma Ata Declaration and the global emphasis on the importance of rural health care. By the late 1980s and early 1990s, as cost-effectiveness became a motivating principle, the policy focus shifted from increasing the number of health workers to improving the efficiency of the

Table 4.1 HRH-Related Plans and Programs

Year	Policy	HRH policy focus
1973–78	First Five-Year Plan	Production of rural health workforce. Significant increases in the production of doctors, but not support staff.
1980–85	Second Five-Year Plan	Introduction of domiciliary health and family planning workers. Production of doctors and medical assistants, with a continued negligence of the production of nurses and midwives.
1985–90	Third Five-Year Plan	Increasing output of medical and dental colleges and the number of nurse training facilities.
1990–95	Fourth Five-Year Plan	Continued focus on increasing the output of health worker training institutions, without attention to strategic staffing or education quality.
1997–2002	Fifth Five-Year Plan	Increasing the production of doctors and nurses. Review and updating of health worker training curriculum. Exposing medical students to community settings. Updating of in-service training materials.
1998–2003	Health and Population Sector Program	
2003–07	National Health Policy	
2003–11	Health, Nutrition, and Population Sector Program	Updating and reviewing job descriptions of DGHS and health worker recruiting rules. Emphasized community orientation in medical curricula.
2008	2008 Health Workforce Strategy and policy on "Transfer and Posting Policy for Officers in Health Service 2008"	Laid out plans to introduce a needs-based human resources plan. Intended to introduce requirement that doctors have two years' minimum service at a union health subcenter.
2011–16	Sixth Five-Year Plan and Health, Population, and Nutrition Sector Development Program	Creation of a midwifery plan. Scaling up the production of health workers, with a particular focus on midwives. Introduction of incentives for service providers to work in remote and hard-to-reach areas and disciplinary measures for absenteeism and misuse of public resources for private gain. Improvements in skill-mix distribution and quality of existing informal and formal sector health workforce. Introduction of a career plan for all cadres of health workers. Integration of alternative care providers into formal health system.

Source: World Bank, adapted from Osman 2013.
Note: DGHS = Directorate General of Health Services.

health workforce through training, education, and a well-designed career plan for all cadres of health workers. In the early 2000s, attention centered on stewardship and governance initiatives, such as developing performance management systems, staff deployment, and HRH information management systems. Most recently, as the Millennium Development Goals deadline of 2015 approaches, the focus is on addressing shortages, the unequal geographic distribution of health workers, and the inappropriate skill-mix.

Despite the efforts and some successes, the problems that still characterize the health workforce highlight the government's inability to design policies to meet the country's HRH challenges, as well as a weak capacity to implement each document's proposals.

And as the government looks to the future, it will need to learn from both these achievements and failures, enabling it to better draft and then put into practice its plans. The focus should be on drafting plans that can be feasibly implemented and ensuring that capacity exists within the MOHFW to follow through with the proposed policies.

First Five-Year Plan (1973–78)

The first Five-Year Plan shifted the focus of health workforce development from curative care in urban areas to community and preventive medicine in rural areas. It created a cadre of home-based health workers called Family Welfare Workers and significantly increased the production of doctors. While these were important developments, the focus on increasing the number of doctors came at the expense of production of nurses and paramedics. This led to the beginning of the inappropriate skill-mix of health workers that continues to be a major challenge in the country today.

Second Five-Year Plan (1980–85)

Under this plan, the relative overproduction of doctors and underproduction of midlevel support staff continued. To meet the newly adopted primary health care targets, a greater focus was placed on producing medical assistants, in addition to doctors. The inappropriate skill-mix began to fully take hold during this period.

Third Five-Year Plan (1985–90)

To begin to address the growing skill-mix problems, the MOHFW began to focus on increasing the output of nurse training facilities, in addition to its continued focus on the production of physicians. However, the focus was more on quantity rather than on the quality of education. The number of training facilities was insufficient to meet the needs and demands of the Bangladeshi population, and health worker shortages persisted. Furthermore, the cumbersome and lengthy government recruitment process did not allow for newly trained health workers to be efficiently absorbed into the public sector health system.

Fourth Five-Year Plan (1990–95)

The focus of health workforce development continued to be on increasing the output of health workers from training facilities. The plan recognized the managerial weaknesses in health workforce planning and set out to create a master plan for the production of different categories of health workers. It also proposed an overhaul of health worker training curricula to address training quality issues that became apparent under the third Five-Year Plan. However, this master plan was never developed or implemented and there was no significant revision in health worker training curriculum. During this period, the doctor-to-population and nurse-to-population ratio increased, but not in a way that strategically addressed geographic or income-based inequalities in the distribution of the health workforce.

Fifth Five-Year Plan (1997–2002), Health and Population Sector Program (1998–2003), and National Health Policy (2000)

Under these policies and programs, the density of both doctors and nurses increased; undergraduate medical, dental, and paramedic curricula were updated; new medical education units were established. The Residential Field Site Program was established to expose medical students to community settings. The in-service training strategy was updated, and field workers received more training. In spite of this clear progress, significant shortcomings in implementation existed.

Skill-mix and geographic distributional issues continued to worsen during this period as a result of a lack of strategic health workforce planning by the MOHFW. Despite the MOHFW's general recognition of a shortage of health workers in rural and underserved areas, it was unable to place doctors in these areas without adequate incentives for posting and retaining health workers in remote areas. Planned improvements in nursing education also did not take place, which further disadvantaged that group of health workers. In general, management within the MOHFW was not equipped to prepare a needs-based HRH Plan and was not strategic in adopting incentives policies to retain health workers in rural areas.

Health, Nutrition, and Population Sector Program (2003–11)

This program focused on improving the efficiency of the health workforce through improved training guidelines that focused on community-oriented medical curricula. In June 2007, the job description of Directorate General of Health Services was completed and the recruitment rules were reviewed and updated. Despite these efforts, there was no substantial change in recruitment, deployment, transfer, or promotion policies in practice. Planned career planning for health workers, as well as performance-based incentive policies were also not implemented. In addition, the job description for nurses remained outdated and in need of review. To make many of the proposed reforms, the MOHFW had to work through the Bangladesh Civil Service codes, which are complicated and lengthy to change. As a result, patronage, nepotism, and corruption were prevalent in the transfer, posting, and promotion procedures.

Health Workforce Strategy and "Transfer and Posting Policy for Officers in Health Service" 2008

Following on the World Development Report 2008, the 2008 Health Workforce Strategy attempted to undertake a needs-based plan for HRH. However, no systematic effort was undertaken, and, as a result, shortages, as well as geographic and skill-mix imbalances, were not addressed. In 2008, the government of Bangladesh adopted a policy where a doctor must serve a minimum of two years at a union health subcenter to be eligible for a more advantageous career ladder. While this policy exists on paper, it has not been implemented and therefore was not effective in addressing geographic imbalances.

The Path to Universal Health Coverage in Bangladesh • http://dx.doi.org/10.1596/978-1-4648-0536-3

The current sixth Five-Year Plan (2011–15), Health, Population, and Nutrition Sector Development Program (2011–16), and 2000 National Health Policy include a common focus on the creation of community-level health workers and formulating a midwifery plan to reduce maternal and infant mortality rates. The policies and programs attempt to address issues of shortages and geographic and skill-mix imbalances through improved training and incentives for service providers. The proposed system includes the application of merit-based incentives as well as disciplinary measures in response to absenteeism or misuse of public sector resources for private gain. They also recognize the need to improve quality of the existing workforce in both the formal and informal sectors by establishing career plans with clear principles for recruitment, promotions, postings, and transfers. Creating clearer standards and licensing of alternative medical care providers has also been included as a component of the Health, Population, and Nutrition Sector Development Program. Similar to the previous policy proposals, these are all laudable goals; however, it is yet to be seen if the government and MOHFW are able to fully implement their proposed plans to effectively address the problems plaguing the health workforce.

A Highly Centralized and Cumbersome Bureaucratic System with Weak Response Capacity

The health system is plagued by overly centralized and bureaucratic decision making, which can lead to delays in policy making and implementation (Ahmed et al. 2013). The process entailed to establish a new post in the MOHFW exemplifies the challenges: six ministries or institutional entities are involved in getting final approval to create a new physician post (see figure 3.4). The MOHFW only initiates the process, after which the Ministry of Public Administration,[2] Ministry of Finance, Committee of Secretaries, Cabinet Ministry, and National Implementation Committee on Administrative Reforms all have to sign off on the new post. This process can take anywhere from six months to two years and does not allow for strategic staffing practices, given the changing needs of the Bangladeshi population.

Similarly, the process to fill a vacancy, even after a physician position has been established in the public sector, can take up to three years, due in part to the multiple government bodies involved. There are at least nine different steps in the approval process, which must pass through the MOHFW, Public Service Commission, and the Ministry of Public Administration (figure 4.1). And so by the time a vacancy has been filled, new vacancies have appeared in the system due to staff turnover, retirement, and expansion of health facilities. This cumbersome process contributes to the roughly 27 percent of all sanctioned physician positions remaining vacant (see chapter 3).

Similar to many other low- and middle-income countries, all HRH-related recruitment, deployment, career progression, and incentive structures are governed by the overall government civil service regulations because all public sector

Figure 4.1 Process to Fill a Vacant Position

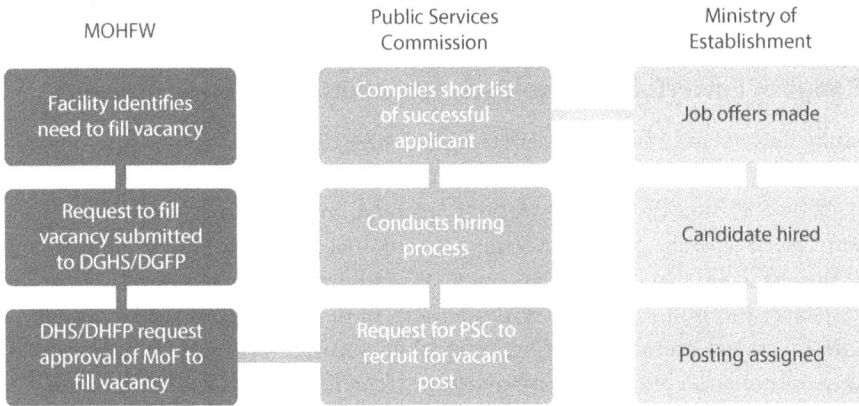

MOHFW	Public Services Commission	Ministry of Establishment
Facility identifies need to fill vacancy	Compiles short list of successful applicant	Job offers made
Request to fill vacancy submitted to DGHS/DGFP	Conducts hiring process	Candidate hired
DHS/DHFP request approval of MoF to fill vacancy	Request for PSC to recruit for vacant post	Posting assigned

Source: World Bank 2010.
Note: DGFP = Directorate General of Family Planning; DGHS = Director General of Health Services; DHS = Demographic and Health Survey; MOHFW = Ministry of Health and Family Welfare.

employees, including health workers, are part of the civil service, leaving their control outside the purview of the MOHFW.

This has several impacts. First, the system is inefficient and leaves it open to the influence of political pressures due to the multitude of government actors involved in decision making. Second, the centralized approach makes it hard to respond to the demands of health facilities, and as such staffing decisions are not necessarily made strategically. Third, given the length of recruitment time, many physicians opt out of the public sector to begin private sector practice, perpetuating the vacancy problems.

Restrictive civil service norms and regulations governing health worker recruitment and salaries have been found to cause delays in hiring and contribute to high vacancy rates in a raft of countries, ranging from Zambia to the Dominican Republic (Vujicic, Ohiri, and Sparkes 2009). One possible way to avoid these issues is to introduce contracting mechanisms that are not subject to overall civil service regulations.

Decisions on establishing new training institutions are subject to this same bureaucratic system. Approval and accreditation of new medical colleges involves the MOHFW, the Bangladesh Medical and Dental College, and Dhaka University, each with its own role (World Bank 2010).

The 2008 Health Workforce Strategy recognized the problems associated with this centralized and bureaucratic system. As part of its strategic objectives, it aims to "have clear lines of accountability with defined roles and responsibilities, and establish performance management at all levels of the system, enabling appropriate delegation of authority to lower levels" (Government of Bangladesh 2008). Without these lines of accountability, there is little capacity to monitor and enforce regulations and policies that are put into place. Similar to other strategic objectives included in plans and programs, the MOHFW needs to work to accomplish this aim.

A Range of Powerful Stakeholders, Some with Competing Interests

To fully understand HRH policy making in Bangladesh, it is important to analyze the range of stakeholders involved and their potential influence, letting us assess the "behavior, intentions, interrelations, agendas, interests, and the influence or resources" of relevant actors concerning a particular policy or issue (Varvasovszky and Brugha 2000). In recent years, such stakeholder analysis has been applied to understand the politics of policy design and implementation in the context of health insurance premiums in Ghana, alcohol control policy in a Russian region, and maternal and child health programs in Uganda (Abiiro and McIntyre 2013; Gil et al. 2010; Gilson et al. 2012; Namazzi et al. 2013; Sarr 2010).

Similar to these policy settings, the development of HRH policy in Bangladesh can be seen as a by-product of the interplay of the different stakeholder interests at distinct points in time. Politicians, development partners, each cadre of health workers, and bureaucrats are just a few of the stakeholder groups that have vested interests in HRH policies and programs. As a result, they have each worked to exert their influence over policy making, which contributes to differing agendas and policy priorities.

The government's willingness to engage with a multiplicity of actors or stakeholder groups, including nongovernmental organizations and the private sector, has led to a pluralistic reform environment for the overall health sector (Das and Horton 2013). These groupings' involvement in setting reform priorities allows for an inclusive policy-making environment, but can complicate policy making and leave it open to political influence.

This subsection analyzes one set of these diverse interests so as to provide insight on how HRH policy has developed in Bangladesh since the 1970s. It highlights the challenges policy makers face when trying to balance potentially divergent interests in addressing the country's ongoing HRH issues. Each of these groups can influence policy at a number of different levels—from setting broad agendas to determining specifics of terms of service and recruitment procedures. This list of five stakeholder groups can also be expanded to include nongovernmental organizations, private sector health workers, and the public at large, to name a few.

Physicians

Physicians are always a powerful interest group in any health system due to their monopoly power over the provision of medical care (Marmor and Thomas 1972). In Bangladesh, physicians exert their influence through the power of the Bangladesh Medical Association (BMA), which is politically connected to the main political parties. The BMA therefore can greatly influence policy decisions that affect the medical profession. For example, while a government committee headed by the MOHFW grants permission to establish institutions for higher medical education, the BMA holds the lone outside seat on the committee. This representation underscores the BMA's power in key decisions on health worker training, which is biased toward physicians.

Additionally, physicians play an important role in setting policy priorities, given their prominent role as high-level government bureaucrats in the MOHFW, ensuring a constant push to increase the number of doctors relative to other health workers since independence in 1971. Physicians have also been able to ensure their ability to engage in both public and private medical practices concurrently. This system of dual practice leads to absenteeism in public facilities, but has remained intact due to potential opposition by the BMA.

Politicians

HRH policy making is an inherently political issue and therefore subject to changes in a country's political climate. Political interests can influence HRH policy making in two ways, by directly affecting health workers' terms of service, and by altering the focus of broader HRH policy priorities. On the first, public sector health workers as government employees are vulnerable to the choices of government actors, including those on service structure, salary, posting, and promotion of physicians in particular. For instance, in recent years, due to political pressure from the BMA, there was a move to create 3,176 physician posts at union level despite a lack of facilities in which to place them.

On the second, politicians' election promises and constituencies can determine policy priorities that are not necessarily based on evidence or a strategic assessment of implementation capacity. For instance, the current government has committed to train 3,000 midwives as an attempt to reduce maternal mortality. Similarly, it has prioritized the creation of CHW posts to support rural health and community clinics. These two political commitments are directly reflected in the sixth Five-Year Plan (2011–15), Health, Population, and Nutrition Sector Development Program (2011–16), and the 2000 National Health Policy, highlighting the importance of political influence in determining HRH policy priorities. Prime Minister Sheikh Hasina's declaration to achieve UHC for all citizens can be seen as another driving force.

While all of these political priorities may contribute to positive outcomes for health, they may also potentially divert resources from more pressing policies. Further, a strong civil society may be needed to hold politicians accountable for their promises and to act as a counterweight to the political influence of the BMA.

Development Partners

Since independence, development partners have played an active, and sometimes dominant, role in HRH policy making. The government has relied heavily on foreign assistance, working closely with donors to develop policies and set priorities. Global trends and international priorities have greatly affected the focus of HRH policy. Donors' influence is derived from their financial support of the health sector, as well as their technical expertise (Ahmed et al. 2013). Before 1997, donor funding for health accounted for around one-third of public population and public health expenditure (Shiffman and Wu 2003). Since 1997, donors have worked directly with the MOHFW to develop programs to complement the country's health policies through its sector-wide approach (SWAp) (see chapter 3), giving them "a seat at the table" to influence policies and allocation of health development resources. In 2012, external resources constituted 7.2 percent of THE (WHO 2014).

Thus, as the country looks to implement policies to achieve UHC, it will have to continue to rely on donor support to ensure the country's health workforce has the capacity to meet the planned increases in demand for health services, compelling HRH policy makers to continue balancing the interests of donors with those of the government and the MOHFW.

Nurses, Other Health Workers, and Informal Providers

Nurses and other cadres of health workers have relatively little power in the health system compared with physicians and do not play an active role in policy making. They are not well organized, partly because they do not have a powerful association to represent their interests, culminating in a lack of voice and hence a severe shortage of nurses and lack of a meaningful career trajectory. The situation is similar for other midlevel health staff and field workers.

Bureaucrats

As seen, due to the highly centralized and bureaucratic nature of the health system, bureaucrats play an important role in setting and implementing policy (Ahmed et al. 2013).

Weak Regulatory and Enforcement Capacity

To fully implement the policies and programs laid out in the various HRH-related policy documents referenced above, the MOHFW needs to have the regulatory and enforcement capacity to fulfill its mandates. However, due to the factors discussed earlier in this chapter, the MOHFW has been unable to put into place regulations that allow for the full implementation of important policies. For instance, despite efforts to increase rural retention and place health workers in remote and hard-to-reach areas, the urban bias of the distribution of health workers persists, as demonstrated by the statistics that the doctor-to-population ratio is 10 times worse in rural than in urban areas (Mabud 2005). This distribution is then exacerbated by high rates of absenteeism in rural areas. The average physician vacancy rate in the country is 33 percent, but only 17 percent in Dhaka (DGHS 2012).

The MOHFW is aware of these issues, but has been unable to effectively monitor or enforce policies to address them. A combination of both regulations and incentives is needed to improve the geographic inequities in the distribution of health workers and reduce absenteeism rates in rural areas.

Another example of the weak regulatory capacity is the MOHFW's inability to stem the pervasive use and presence of unqualified health workers by Bangladeshis. As of 2007, informal sector providers constituted 88 percent of all health care providers (HCPs) in the country (Ahmed et al. 2009). These unqualified providers are the primary source of health care for Bangladeshis in some remote areas of the country (Mahmood et al. 2010). The government has failed to stop pervasive use of these providers and is pursuing plans to try to better integrate them into the formal health care system.

Conclusions

Bangladesh has had an active HRH policy-making environment since gaining independence in the early 1970s. In that time, the government has worked to address HRH challenges through its broader strategic planning and health sector-related policies and programs. However, these policies have not been effective in tackling these HRH-related challenges. In addition to the lack of effectiveness of these policies and programs, the HRH policy-making process is also subject to the political influence of stakeholder and interest groups that can result in a lack of strategic planning and potentially incorrect policy priorities.

The overly cumbersome, bureaucratic and centralized system leaves space for these stakeholder groups to insert their influence at a number of different points in the policy-making process. This system also makes it difficult for the MOHFW to effectively implement reforms to the health workforce due to the multiple government entities required to sign off on any policy changes. This burdensome system does not provide for clear lines of accountability, resulting in a low capacity to both implement and enforce policy reforms. These complicated processes and institutional arrangements contribute to the ongoing HRH challenges and will need to be addressed as part of Bangladesh's broader policy efforts to achieve UHC in the coming years.

Notes

1. See appendix B.
2. Formerly, Ministry of Establishment.

CHAPTER 5

HRH Policy Options for UHC

Introduction

To reach its goal of universal health coverage (UHC) by 2032, the government will have to commit itself to policies to strengthen its health workforce. Given the relatively fragmented nature of the country's health system, policy makers in both the health and nonhealth sectors will be required to act. Below are different policy options to address the key human resources for health (HRH) challenges for the government to consider:

Address HRH Shortages

The shortage of health care providers (HCPs) is well recognized. With only 30 percent of the World Health Organization (WHO)-recommended level of 25 qualified HCPs per 10,000 population to reach the Millennium Development Goals (MDGs), absolute numbers of HCPs need to be increased to make progress toward UHC. However, recruitment delays and problems in filling sanctioned posts mean that newly trained health workers are not adequately recruited into the health system.

The following strategies may help reduce the HRH shortage:

Accelerate filling current vacancies. The first step in addressing the shortage of HCPs is to fill currently available and vacant positions, from paramedic/field workers to physicians, particularly cadres where HCP supply is sufficient. The Ministry of Health and Family Welfare (MOHFW) needs to engage other ministries and local authorities to improve coordination and the overall hiring process. At its level, the MOHFW also needs to focus on improving the efficiency in the hiring process to ensure timely hiring of qualified and unemployed health workers.

Accelerate the recruitment of nurses and community health workers (CHWs) and introduce a comprehensive HRH master plan. A modeling exercise assessed the feasibility of different HCP scaling-up scenarios (appendix C). Taking into consideration current staffing structures, HCP training and production capacities, total MOHFW staff salaries, and the fiscal threshold for hiring additional HCPs until 2021, three feasible scenarios are explored. All three assume using 100 percent of the potential fiscal threshold available for physicians, nurses, and CHWs, but each scenario aims at achieving a different physician: nurse: CHW ratio (table 5.1).

Scenario II is probably the most feasible as it will absorb almost all graduates of nursing schools (figure 5.1). However, this scenario will allow the recruitment of only 13 percent of graduating doctors. Also, the low projected costs in the early years (until 2016) will not translate into savings that can be used to cover the HCPs until 2021. Therefore, the MOHFW should explore budgetary channels outside the government's revenue budget to provide funding for additional

Table 5.1 Three Scenarios for Additional HCPs until 2021

	Number of additional HCPs by 2021				Physician: nurse CHW ratio
	Physicians	Nurses	CHWs	Total	
Scenario I	9,212	7,029	7,012	23,253	1:1:1
Scenario II	6,620	13,397	4,420	24,437	1:1.5:1
Scenario III	4,609	18,336	2,409	25,354	1:2:1

Source: World Bank.
Note: CHW = Community health worker; HCP = Health care provider.

Figure 5.1 Scenario II: Recruitment of Additional HCPs to Reach a Physician: Nurse: CHW Ratio of 1:1.5:1 by 2021

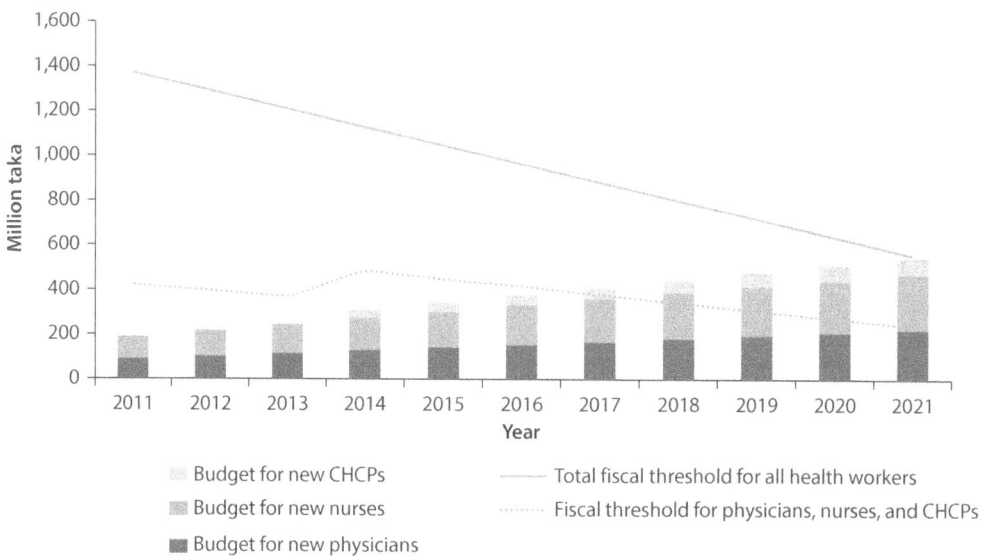

Source: World Bank.
Note: CHCP = Community Health Care Provider.

positions—the sooner this is done, the better. The current sector-wide approach (SWAp) may be a vehicle for financing the recruitment of nurses and CHWs to accelerate closing the gap. Experience from Ethiopia showed that one effective strategy can be to recruit HCPs using direct project aid and then later to move these line items to the MOHFW (Dayrit, Dolea, and Dreesch 2011). Kenya's "Emergency Hiring Plan," which used donor funds to rapidly scale up the health workforce is another good example (box 5.1). By adopting this strategy, the MOHFW will not require interministerial approvals that cause delays in creating new positions.

Box 5.1 Kenya: An Emergency Hiring Plan to Rapidly Scale Up the Health Workforce

In the early 2000s, Kenya faced a severe health workforce shortage as a result of a restrictive public sector wage bill and a lengthy public sector recruitment process (Vujicic, Ohiri, and Sparkes 2009). The Ministry of Health (MOH) estimated a shortage of 7,773 health professionals across five cadres, ranging from nurse to clinical officer (Fogarty and Adano 2009). However, despite these vacancies, Kenya also had a large pool of unemployed health workers. Faced with a growing human immunodeficiency virus/acquired immune deficiency syndrome (HIV/AIDS) burden, the government of Kenya sought to rapidly scale up its health workforce.

The Emergency Hiring Plan (EHP) was developed collaboratively between the MOH and a consortium of donors, including the Clinton Foundation, U.S. Agency for International Development (USAID), and the Global Fund to Fight AIDS, Tuberculosis and Malaria (Vujicic, Ohiri, and Sparkes 2009). Donor funds were used to cover the hiring costs and remuneration of health personnel on three-year contracts tied to specific geographic locations (Gross et al. 2010). These health workers were employed by the MOH and received the same salaries and allowances as regular hires, except—as they were not part of the civil service—they received an additional 31 percent of their base salary in lieu of pension payments. Under the EHP, hiring authority was transferred from the Public Service Commission to the MOH, and the recruitment process was computerized.

As a result of the plan, the time lag between posting a position and an accepted candidate beginning work fell from 18 months to less than 5 months (Adano 2008). By 2006, 83 percent of 3,000 new MOH health workers had been hired under the EHP. A longitudinal study measuring the impact of the program found that the EHP contributed to a 12 percent increase in the number of public sector nurses, who were subsequently absorbed by the government civil service by 2010 (Gross et al. 2010). In addition to its success in rapidly filling vacancies, the EHP was also able to retain 94 percent of all hires as of 2008 (Fogarty and Adano 2009).

The success of the EHP in recruiting and retaining health workers can be attributed to (i) a fair and transparent recruitment process; (ii) adequate training of workers; (iii) regular and timely payments; (iv) recruitment of local candidates; and (v) assignment of posts according

box continues next page

Box 5.1   Kenya: An Emergency Hiring Plan to Rapidly Scale Up the Health Workforce *(continued)*

to geographical preference (Fogarty and Adano 2009; Intrahealth 2009). Through this public/private partnership, the EHP was able to rapidly scale up Kenya's health workforce while allowing the government time to mobilize resources to eventually absorb the short-term contracted health workers into the civil service.

Source: World Bank.

In addition, the MOHFW needs to have a master plan for HRH to guide the recruitment of new HCPs including physicians, nurses, and other HCPs for both short (10 years) and long (20 years) terms, which can be based on the modeling detailed in appendix C.

Make working in the public sector more attractive. The MOHFW, with the Ministry of Finance and Ministry of Public Administration, should consider using financial and nonfinancial incentives to attract health workers into the public sector. Incentive structures and performance bonuses should be carefully assessed to be able to attract both unemployed and potential health workers, as many health workers are either not working in the health sector or are employed in the private sector. Studies should be conducted to ensure that remuneration levels are appropriately set to entice these workers into the public health sector. For example, provider payments under the Maternal Voucher Scheme were not sufficient to persuade private providers to participate, and therefore the full objectives of the program were not met (Bangladesh Health Watch 2012).

Explore contracting mechanisms with nonstate service providers. The MOHFW should explore contracting mechanisms with nonstate providers to supplement the public HCP network. It will need to rely on the 68 percent of all physicians working in the private sector to meet the expected increased demand from expanding health coverage. It already had experience in contracting nongovernmental organizations (NGOs) for nutrition and HIV/AIDS services, which can be built on to strengthen the contract management function. A relevant example is Afghanistan's strategy to form partnerships with NGOs, which has led to higher quality of care for the poor (Hansen et al. 2008).

Regulate dual practice for public sector health workers. The MOHFW needs to take steps to regulate and enforce dual practice norms. With 80 percent of all public sector physicians engaged in dual practice, there is potential for misuse of the system (ICDDR,B 2010). Given the absolute shortage of physicians in the public sector, the MOHFW needs to put into place strict regulations to ensure they are meeting their public sector requirements before working in the private sector. Furthermore, performance payments can be structured to incentivize more physicians to work full time in the public sector. Turkey was successful in reducing the proportion of physicians engaged in dual practice from 89 percent to less than 20 percent between 2002 and 2010 through a mixture of financial incentives and the stricter enforcement of regulations (Evans 2013; Vujicic, Ohiri, and Sparkes 2009). Another approach is to establish "private wings" in public hospitals in which public providers can operate. However, these options should be balanced to tackle underlying causes, such as incentives and accountability structures (Araujo, Mahat, and Lemiere 2014).

Engage other government entities to expedite the hiring process. Nine government entities are involved in recruiting public sector employees. The MOHFW needs to engage in a dialogue at cabinet level to highlight the HRH crisis and its impact on impeding the prime minister's vision for UHC and for the Public Service Commission to give priority and expedite hiring of HCPs. Standardized deadlines and timetables should be strictly enforced. The government should reevaluate its mandatory retirement age of 59 for all public sector workers, as it is losing experienced providers.

Establish high-level coordination platforms in the MOHFW. The MOHFW should implement the planned National Health Workforce Committee and National Professional Standards Committee as laid out in the Health Workforce Strategy for 2012–32. These entities should be responsible for leading the coordinated effort to train, recruit, deploy, and regulate all HCPs in the country, so as to set workload standards that should increase the role of nurses, midwives, and paraprofessionals. This type of country coordinating body has been shown to be effective in creating an effective HRH information system in Sudan (Badr et al. 2013). In addition, the National Health Workforce Committee may be tasked with improving coordination between the Ministry of Local Government, Rural Development and Cooperation and the MOHFW to fill existing vacancies. Successful strategies in other countries include a bundle of interventions, including greater social and community support, embedded within broader multisector development actions, as in Chile, Indonesia, Thailand, and Zambia (Lehmann, Dieleman, and Martineau 2008; Peña et al. 2010).

Improve the Skill-Mix

The MOHFW needs to reverse the current ratio of 2.5 physicians for every nurse and midwife. This imbalance leads to an inefficient use of resources, where nurses, midwives, and paramedics could fulfill many tasks that are currently done by physicians. Strategies should be the following:

Introduce task shifting. As recruitment for physicians is a slow task, shifting of some of the doctors' tasks to other HCPs would be a viable option. In the United Kingdom and in Australia, nurses are allowed to prescribe medicines (WHO 2010a), whereas auxiliary HCPs like CHWs, nurse aids, traditional birth attendants, and medical assistants are an integral part of the health workforce in many national health systems including Malawi, Tanzania, Ghana, Argentina, Brazil, Ethiopia, and Mozambique (Araujo and Maeda 2013). This would require a careful assessment of the current workload of existing HCPs and initiate the process of increasing staff positions for recruitment. It is particularly pertinent for the workload capacities of nurses, paramedics, and fieldworkers. Standard tools are available to conduct this assessment, such as the WHO's Workload Indicators of Staffing Needs process (WHO 2010a). The MOHFW needs to work with the Bangladesh Medical Association and the Nursing Association to carve out specific tasks that nurses can take on. By approaching this process in a collaborative manner, the MOHFW should be able to get the buy-in and input from physicians to increase the role played by nurses and other cadres in the health system.

Improve the stature of nurses and midwives. Social stigma against treatment by nurses and midwives can be reduced by informing the public of the vital role they play. A public education campaign is needed to promote and improve the stature of nurses and midwives, which should increase demand for training. Another effective approach to promote the status of different health care cadres, as seen in Cuba, is the government's active role in training and exporting of health professionals to other countries (Reed 2010). The MOHFW should also promote women working after marriage to retain trained nurses and nurse-midwives through broader social messaging campaigns. It does not have the discretion to raise the base salaries of HCPs because these salaries are set by the Ministry of Public Administration. Therefore, as part of the overall Health Workforce Strategy for 2012–32, efforts should be made by the cabinet to explore the most appropriate salary to maximize health worker retention while maintaining fiscal prudence.

Increase production capacity for nurses. To achieve a better skill-mix of doctor-to-nurse ratio of 1:2 (scenario III, appendix C), the existing production capacity of nurses needs to be increased by 10 percent a year for the next 10 years. The MOHFW needs to increase the number of seats available to train nurses in public sector institutions. The MOHFW can work to provide licenses and accreditation for these institutions, while incentivizing students to enroll. Additional reasons for increasing the number of nurses include the fact that the cost per nurse is much lower than (only half of) the cost per doctor; nurses' job satisfaction is higher than physicians' in Bangladesh (World Bank 2003); recruitment rates for nurses are higher than for physicians (Bangladesh Health Watch 2008); nurses are more likely to work in rural areas (Bangladesh Health Watch 2008), where the workforce shortage is much more severe; and there are positive correlations between the nurse-to-physician ratio and health outcomes (Ahmed, Hossain et al. 2011; Bigbee 2008). In Bangladesh, Khulna is the only division where there is a higher nurse-to-physician ratio and is showing better health service utilization and health outcome indicators (figures 5.2 and 5.3).

Train new cadres of community skilled birth attendants and midwives. The MOHFW should train new health workers as community skilled birth attendants and not only pull from the existing health workforce to fill these roles. A similar training program should be instituted for midwife training that creates a new cadre of health workers that does not only take from already trained nurses. The current system depletes the already scarce number of nurses available to fulfill other roles. More people can be served by increasing the number of nurses, midwives, and paraprofessionals and concurrently increase their roles and responsibilities. Evidence

Figure 5.2 Physician-to-Nurse Ratio and Health Service Utilization by Division

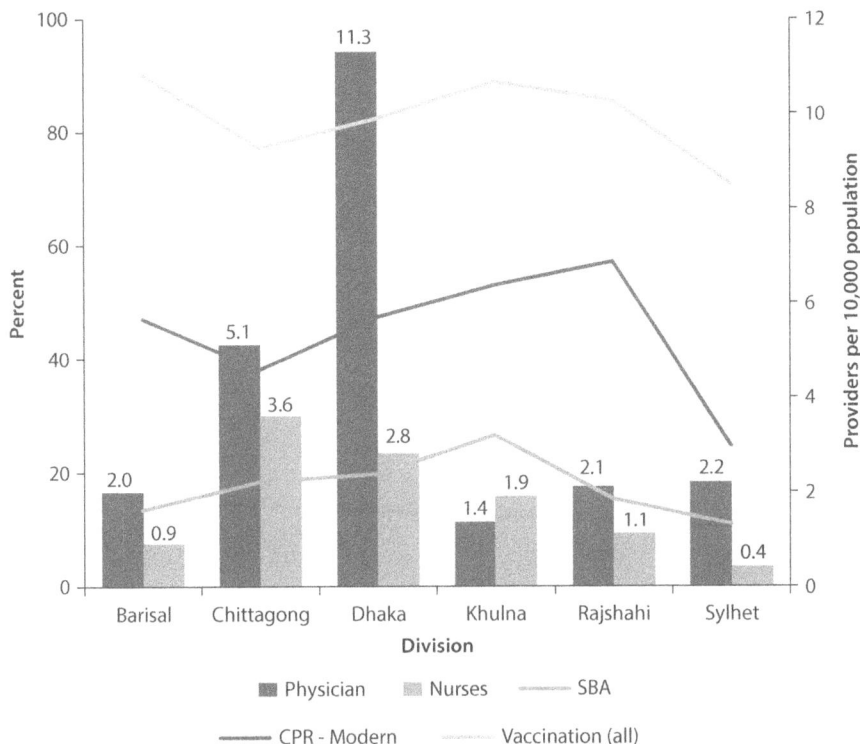

Sources: Bangladesh Health Watch 2008, p. 9 (table 2.2); Bangladesh Demographic and Health Survey (BDHS) 2007.
Note: SBA= Skilled birth attendance (not attendant); CPR= Contraceptive Prevalence Rate.

from Afghanistan (presented in box 5.2) demonstrates how new cadres of nurses and midwives contribute in rebuilding the primary care and emergency services (Acerra et al. 2009) and in increasing skilled birth attendance (Mohmand 2013). Bangladesh itself provides a successful example of the effective use of CHWs for TB control and treatment under BRAC (May, Rhatigan, and Cash 2011).

Create new cadres of health workers to supplement formal HCPs. The MOHFW should train and use CHWs to provide basic services and act as an extension of the formal health sector. In addition to recognizing basic symptoms, these health workers can administer essential treatments and engage in prevention activities at the community level. They should be considered an integral part of the overall health system and given well-defined roles and responsibilities. This will involve close coordination with NGOs in rural areas that provide funding for many CHWs. Malawi, for example, has shown significant scale-up of HIV/AIDS service delivery across all levels of the health system by increasing the number of lower trained HCP cadres (Brugha et al. 2010), and Ethiopia increased its coverage of health services through the Health Extension Worker program (El-Saharty et al. 2009). Similarly, Nepal has introduced a range of trained health workers to link the community with the health system (box 5.3).

Figure 5.3   Physician-to-Nurse Ratio and Health Outcomes by Division

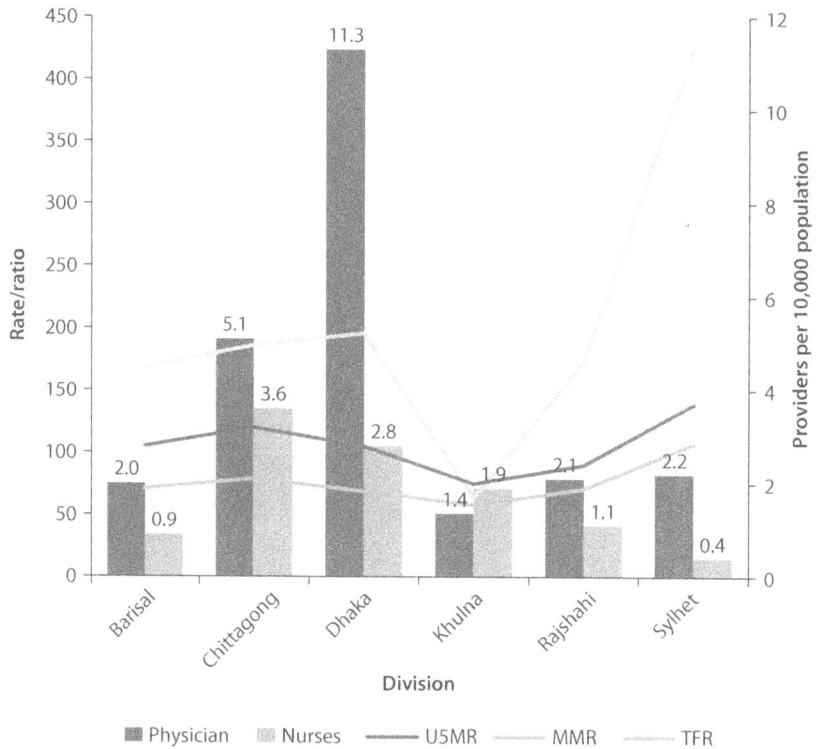

Sources: Bangladesh Health Watch 2008, p. 9 (table 2.2); NIPORT et al. 2009; and NIPORT et al. 2012.
Note: MMR = Maternal mortality ratio; U5MR= Under-Five Mortality Rate; TFR = Total Fertility Rate.

Box 5.2   Afghanistan: Community Midwifery Education Program

Afghanistan's health services in the immediate postconflict period were in a deplorable state: its 2002 maternal mortality ratio (MMR), for example, was the second highest in the world, reflecting lack of access to and utilization of reproductive health services and skilled care during pregnancy, childbirth, and the first month after delivery. In a society where women seek care only from female providers, the lack of qualified female health workers in remote areas seriously restricts service utilization. In 2003, most Afghan women delivered at home, and fewer than 10 percent of births were attended by a skilled provider. Very few midwives were willing to work in rural areas, and there were no training facilities and very few qualified female graduates in the provinces. Given the dire situation, urgent action had to be taken to address the shortage of midwives.

The Community Midwifery Education (CME) Program was established in 2003, aiming not only to train more midwives but also to ensure both their initial deployment to remote health facilities as well as their retention. These aims were realized through the creation of a new health cadre known as "community midwives." The five-step framework of the CME Program, that is, recruitment, admission, curriculum and training, accreditation, and deployment and

box continues next page

Box 5.2 Afghanistan: Community Midwifery Education Program *(continued)*

retention, contains innovative designs and their rigorous implementation and is enhanced by strong stakeholder engagement and community involvement throughout the process. For example, admission is based on national admission policy and criteria, including an entrance exam. The program curriculum has been standardized and entails two years of training. Accreditation, administered by the National Midwifery Education Accreditation Board, has played an important role in improving the quality of care provided by midwives.

As a result of the program, the number of midwives has increased markedly—in 2003, there were only 467 midwives in Afghanistan; by April 2013, 2,245 students had graduated as community midwives. Their training and deployment helped improve access to and use of reproductive health services. Antenatal care (ANC) utilization, for example, appears to have more than tripled during the period 2003–10. The increased access to services was especially marked in rural Afghanistan. Challenges still remain—including influence peddling (including the use of force) by local potentates, the lack of eligible students in some targeted communities, accreditation of the CME schools in provinces where security is a problem, and the lack of a national tracking system for CME-graduated midwives. The Ministry of Public Health (MoPH) considers the program a successful intervention and will undertake its replication to tackle the shortage of other human resources for health.

Source: Adapted from Mohmand 2013.

Box 5.3 Nepal: Trained Outreach Workers Linking the Community to the Health System

In setting up its primary health care system in the 1980s, the government of Nepal established a range of community health workers, which included village health workers (VHWs), maternal child health workers (MCHWs), and female community health volunteers (FCHVs). Each health post, subhealth post, or primary health care center, serving a catchment population between 5,000 and 10,000, has a minimum of one professional health worker as a facility in-charge as well as one VHW, one MCHW, and nine FCHVs.

VHWs and MCHWs are literate, paid, locally recruited, and provided training. They work full-time and spend part of their time providing services at health post/subhealth post and part of their time providing services from outreach delivery sites. They are responsible for providing a range of maternal and child health interventions, family planning, and other services. VHWs are responsible for supervising and supporting FCHVs. FCHVs are volunteers and a nationally recognized cadre of health workers. They are selected from their communities and are responsible for 100 to 150 households. They receive incentives for different aspects of their work and typically work four to eight hours a week, providing a diverse array of services, including dosing vitamin A for children, antenatal counseling, commodity distribution, and case management. FCHVs are also supervised by other community health workers in their own communities, which creates accountability and improves retention.

box continues next page

Coordinate training activities. To improve the skill-mix distribution and promote task shifting, the government should work with the Bangladesh Technical Education Board to coordinate training. This will ensure that trainees are given the appropriate skills to complete their required tasks once they have finished their education. The nurse and nurse-midwife training curriculum should be upgraded across the education system, with direct ties to in-service training activities.

Address Geographic Imbalances

Interventions are needed to improve the distribution of HCPs between rural and urban areas.

Introduce targeted training programs for community and traditional health workers. The MOHFW should train informal sector health workers to act as conduits between patients and the formal health system. These community and traditional health workers are the primary point of contact with the health system for many Bangladeshis living in rural areas (Mahmood et al. 2010). Targeted training activities have been shown to be effective in identifying serious illness and referring patients to the formal health system in Bangladesh (Hamid et al. 2006; Sarma and Oliveras 2011). However, this should be done in regions that suffer from extreme shortages of HCPs and only for a limited time until enough qualified HCPs are mobilized.

Establish regional training institutions. The MOHFW needs to create training institutions in rural areas and use careful examination requirements for rural trainees to maximize the likelihood of their staying in these areas once they complete training. One particular issue that can be addressed is the current science requirement to enter medical school. The MOHFW can set up a preparatory science course for students in rural areas who have not received this training prior to entering medical school. By placing institutions in these rural areas and recruiting from local populations, trainees may be more likely to practice there as HCPs, as seen in countries like China, the Democratic Republic of Congo, Japan, and the United States (Dolea, Stormont, and Braichet 2010; WHO 2010a). Coupled with setting up training institutions in rural areas, the MOHFW should also design continuing education and professional development programs that meet the needs of rural health workers and are accessible from where they live and work, so as to support their retention (WHO 2010a).

Implement mandatory service requirements. The current mandatory service requirements in the public sector should be expanded and enforced. The MOHFW should ensure that rural classifications are accurate. Rural service should also be required for professional licensing. Physicians should have to practice a minimum of one to two years in a rural area before becoming fully licensed. These requirements should be strictly enforced. Such interventions are in place in more than 70 countries (Frehywot et al. 2010); the example of Thailand's integrated interventions is presented in box 5.4.

Box 5.4 Thailand: Integrated Interventions Enhance Equitable Distribution of Physicians Nationally

Between 1960 and 2002, Thailand introduced a series of initiatives to address the inequitable distribution of physicians in the country. These programs set out specifically to reduce the migration of physicians to urban areas and to foreign countries and to increase the number of physicians serving in rural areas.

Beginning in 1968, the government of Thailand introduced a bundle of interventions to attract doctors to work in rural areas. These included compulsory three-year public service, hardship allowances, rural recruitment and hometown placement strategies for medical colleges, and public recognition awards for rural physicians.

The government's targeted programs to improve the stature and distribution of physicians in rural areas led to an increase in the number of rural doctors from 300 in 1976 to 1,162 in 1985. In 1979, the population-to-doctor ratio of Thailand's least developed region was 21.3 times higher than that of Bangkok, and by 1986 it had dropped to just 8.6 times higher. Despite these earlier successes, Thailand suffered reverses between 1987 and 1993, with physicians moving from the public to the private sector. This trend diminished some of the gains that had been made in previous years. However, with the Asian financial crisis in 1997 doctors began serving in rural facilities once again. A recent study showed that graduates recruited through the special track (from rural backgrounds) had a 10–15 percent higher probability of fulfilling the mandatory service. These graduates also scored higher on four out of five competencies, notably procedural skills, but normal track graduates had higher competency on clinical knowledge in major clinical subjects.

This bundle of interventions to attract physicians to rural service helped to rebalance the distribution of physicians and led to an increase in the number and proportion of rural physicians during the rural health development period and after the 1997 financial crisis. However, had the interventions been more proactive and better integrated, they would have produced far more substantive gains in addressing geographic imbalances.

Source: Wilbulpolprasert and Pengpaibon 2003; Noree, Chokchaichan, and Mongkolporn 2005; Putthasri et al. 2013.

Table 5.2 Deployment of New Recruits by Region

Region	Total population (thousands)	Rate per 100,000 population		Nurse-to-doctor ratio	Distriblution of new recruits until 2021		
		Doctors	Nurses		Doctors	Nurses	CHWs
Sylhet	9,808	2.2	0.4	0.18	454	5,511	1,818
Dhaka	46,729	10.8	2.8	0.26	1,322	1,250	413
Rajshahi	18,329	2.1	1.1	0.52	1,334	2,497	824
Barisal	8,147	1.7	0.9	0.53	488	2,035	671
Chittagong	28,079	4.8	3.6	0.75	1,192	877	289
Kuhlna	15,562	1.3	1.9	1.46	1,829	1,227	405
Total	126,654				6,620	13,397	4,420

Source: World Bank.

Introduce targeted recruitment practices. The MOHFW should use targeted recruitment policies (for example, local recruitment for various health disciplines), particularly for nurse and paramedic/fieldworker positions, to increase the likelihood of retention in rural areas (WHO 2010a). As suggested above, scenario II (detailed in appendix C) is probably the most feasible for increasing the number of HCPs. Detailed deployment data under this scenario are in table 5.2. Most nurses and CHWs will be deployed to Sylhet, Rajshahi, and Barisal.

Retain Health Workers

Health workers must be retained by the health system, entailing a raft of strategies:

Augment the pool of HCPs. A first step for the MOHFW to increase numbers of health workers is to draw health workers employed in the nonhealth sector back into the health sector through financial and nonfinancial incentives. Many Bangladeshis trained as health professionals have opted out of the health workforce due to better opportunities or problems with working outside the home for women. Health workers with a rural background are more likely to stay and practice in rural areas after completing their studies, at least in countries such as Indonesia and Thailand (Araujo and Maeda 2013).

Establish a placement system for trainees. A pipeline for trainees should be created while they are still in school, so that they can immediately enter public health service, without recruitment delays. The MOHFW should work with training institutions to identify these candidates and ensure their placement.

Create a clear career development system. The MOHFW should unify the career progression pathways between different directorates, particularly for nurses to improve their retention, which will involve coordinated in-service training and differential pay grades.

Establish an incentive system for public sector HCPs. The MOHFW should use a combination of financial and nonfinancial incentives to retain HCPs in the public system and encourage them to serve in rural and remote areas. A well-coordinated performance-based system can provide additional funds for HCPs to keep them in the public sector, particularly in underserved areas. For example, incentives such as social prestige, positive community feedback, feeling needed in their jobs, and career progression have been shown to be effective in retaining CHWs and inducing them to take on a greater workload in Bangladesh (Alam, Tasneem, and Oliveras 2012a, 2012b; Rahman et al. 2010). Several countries, including Thailand, Zambia, Mozambique, Kenya, and Chile, have taken initiatives to provide incentives outside the salaries and payments to improve retention, which include government housing to staff (Araujo and Maeda 2013), as well as lower car loan rates and scholarships to send children to better schools in Zambia (Lehmann, Dieleman, and Martineau 2008). Performance incentives to practice in rural areas have been successful in retaining physicians in rural areas in Thailand (Tangcharoensathien et al. 2013). Donor funds can be channeled for this purpose. Therefore, interministerial budgetary approvals are not required to allocate the additional funds needed to pay the performance bonuses. Malawi has channeled donor resources for this purpose to pay performance bonuses for HCPs (Bowie, Mwase, and Chinkhumba 2009). The example from Chile is presented in box 5.5.

Box 5.5 Chile: Well-Designed Incentive Package Successfully Addressed Physician Retention

Like many countries, Chile has struggled to keep health workers from migrating from rural to urban areas or out of Chile entirely. The Rural Practitioner Program (RPP) was initiated in Chile in 1955 with the objective of attracting and retaining health workers in underserved areas.

Physicians under the RPP work in rural primary care hospitals and health clinics between three to six years. Participants are offered attractive financial incentives, including a paid residency in a university hospital with a competitive salary and benefits that escalate with the degree of isolation and job responsibilities. They also receive nonfinancial incentives, such as four-week rural clerkships, opportunities to participate in managerial activities, and professional development training. Financing for the RPP is guaranteed by a 1963 law that requires the allocation of public resources according to the total number of program positions.

According to a study using Chilean Ministry of Health data, between 2000 and 2008 the RPP was able to fill 100 percent of available positions, at a retention rate of nearly 100 percent over the three-year assignment. However, the RPP was less successful in retaining physicians beyond the three-year minimum period and by the end of the sixth year the retention rate fell to 58 percent. Participants reported high rates (90 percent) of satisfaction with the RPP, and 70 percent planned to pursue specialization in their referred hospital. Researchers found that the RPP was effective in aligning individual physicians' interests in specialization with the health services needs in underserved remote areas. A blend of incentives, both financial and nonfinancial, was key in attracting and retaining graduate physicians.

Source: Adapted from Peña et al. 2010.

Adopt Strategic Payment and Purchaser Mechanisms

Payment mechanisms should incentivize performance from both public and private sector providers. The MOHFW has experience with strategic purchasing and performance-based systems through the Maternal Voucher Scheme, so the concept is not completely new.

However, careful analysis will need to be conducted to set payment levels if these mechanisms are to be expanded to general health services. The MOHFW will also have to ensure that user fee revenues are replaced for public sector providers. One potential source of additional revenues to pay providers is donor funds. While they may not necessarily fund the base salaries of providers, a pool may be created to pay performance incentives to both public and private sector providers. This system was implemented under a SWAp in Malawi to provide top-ups to public sector providers (Carlson et al. 2008). Additionally, the MOHFW and National Health Security Office will need to rely on private sector providers to meet the increased demand that UHC should bring to the health system. Private sector contracting mechanisms, such as those used in Turkey, may effectively fill gaps in public sector provision, particularly in rural and hard-to-reach areas.

Establish a Central Human Resources Information System

The MOHFW needs to establish a central Human Resources Information System (HRIS) to strengthen and coordinate with the existing director general–level personnel management and information systems to produce real-time human resources scenarios by geographic regions and to feed into the MOHFW's decision making and policy development. Without this coordinated and centralized system, the MOHFW's current endeavor to formulate its HRH strategy will not be implementable. This intervention has been shown to be effective in Peru, where a centralized HRIS led to strengthened stewardship of the MOHFW over human resources development (Dayrit, Dolea, and Dreesch 2011).

Target HRH Interventions to Improve Maternal and Newborn Health

The MOHFW will have to engage in targeted interventions to improve HRH capacities in these areas. First, it should train and deploy all cadres of health personnel, including community-based skilled birth attendants, in teams to small facilities to meet the goal of increasing skilled birth attendant coverage by 30 percent by 2015. This approach would scale up access to these services 10 times faster than deploying individual health workers for home deliveries. Second, before increasing comprehensive Emergency Obstetric Care (EmOC) facilities at upazila and union levels, it may be more effective for the MOHFW to invest first in the 62 district and general hospitals and 22 medical colleges so they can provide comprehensive EmOC 24 hours a day, 7 days a week (Koblinsky et al. 2008).

Health Coverage and Service Delivery System

Public Service Delivery System

Public sector health services reflect the country's administrative levels—national, divisional, district, upazila (subdistrict), union, and ward—with the Ministry of Health and Family Welfare (MOHFW) responsible for implementing, managing, coordinating, and regulating national health and family planning–related activities, programs, and policies. The MOHFW delivers health services directly through its own facilities under the direction of two separate executing authorities: the Directorates of Health Services (DGHS) and the Directorate of Family Planning (DGFP) (figure A.1).

As of 2010, the MOHFW intended to move toward a facility-based delivery system with the Essential Services Package (ESP) delivered by an integrated team of health and family planning personnel (World Bank 2010). Under this system, the first point of contact with the health system would be in community clinics at the ward level, with referrals to union and upazila facilities. Current doorstep services would be replaced with fixed-site services.

The health service delivery system is organized into public, not-for-profit (nongovernmental organization [NGO]), and for-profit private sectors. The public sector has by far the largest infrastructure in the country, extending to the lowest administrative unit, that is, wards (with an approximate population of 6,000). The public sector is largely used for in-patient and preventive care, while the private sector (a heterogeneous group differing in their training, legal status, system of medicine used, and type of organization) is used mainly for outpatient curative care (World Bank 2003).

In the public sector, primary-level health care consists of upazila health complexes (UZHCs), with in-patient (31 beds) and basic laboratory facilities. They are supported by subcenters such as the union/rural subcenters under the DGHS and union health and family welfare centers (UHFWCs) under the DGFP, and a network of community clinics (CCs) at ward level. In the sector-wide approach

Figure A.1   Public Service Delivery System

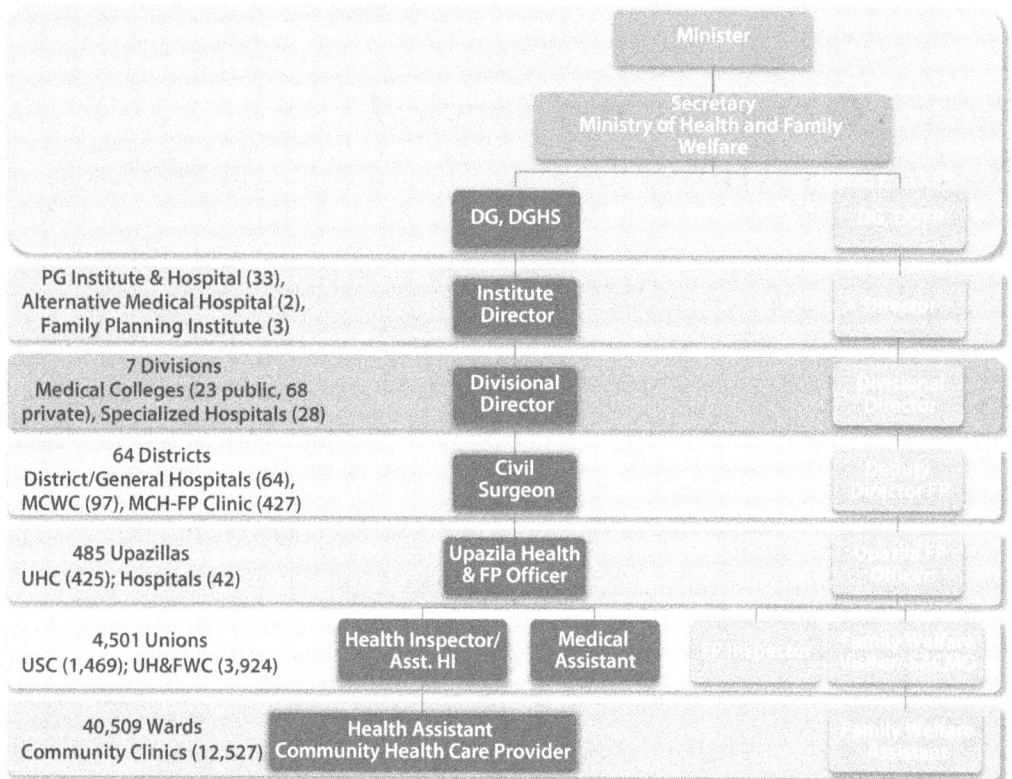

Source: Management Information System-Directorate General of Health Services 2014.
Note: DG = Directorate General; DGHS = Directorate General of Health Services; DGFP = Directorate General of Family Planning; FP = Family Planning; HI = Health Inspector; MCH-FP = Maternal Child Health and Family Planning; MCWC = Maternal and Child Welfare Center; MOHFW = Ministry of Health and Family Welfare; PG = Postgraduate; SACMO = Sub-assistant Community Medical Officer; UHC = Universal health coverage; UHFWC = Union Health and Family Welfare Center.

(SWAp), adopted in 1998, a basic package of essential health care is provided from the primary health care (PHC) centers.

In urban areas, the Ministry of Local Government, Rural Development and Cooperatives is primarily responsible for all public health service delivery. As these urban areas do not receive funding from the government, and health service delivery is paid for by local government revenues and NGO funding (USAID Bangladesh 2011), public facilities in urban areas have many health worker vacancies and are generally underfunded.

Nonstate actors play an important role in health care delivery with respect to their share of total utilization and expenditures. Due to the poor performance of the public health sector, the Medical Practice and Private Clinics and Laboratories Ordinance was promulgated in 1982 to encourage the growth of private health care service delivery to increase competition and introduce market forces into the health system (Andaleeb 2000). As a result, there was a large increase in private hospitals and clinics registered with the Directorate of Hospitals and

Clinics in the 1980s and 1990s. This vibrant private health sector remains in place today, and the government is working to promote partnerships between the private and public sectors (World Bank 2010).

Staffing of Primary Health Care Centers

Staff at different levels of PHC facilities, for example, UZHC, Universal Health Coverages, health centers/union health and family welfare centers, and community clinics are shown in table A.1. A mixed cadre of health workers is involved in the delivery of services at each level of PHC facilities. Posting in rural areas and rural retention of health care provides (HCPs) is problematic and discussed below.

Table A.1 Staff Mix at Upazila Level and Below in the Formal Sector

Facility	Staff—health		Staff—family planning	
Upazila health complex	Upazila health and family planning officer, head of UHC	1	Upazila family planning officer	1
			Assistant upazila family planning officer	
	Junior consultant gynecology	1	*Clinical service:*	
	Junior consultant surgery	1	Medical officer	1
	Junior consultant medicine	1	MCH officer	1
	Junior consultant anesthetics	1	Family welfare visitor	1
	Residential medical officer	1		
	General medical officers	1		
	Dental surgeon	1		
	Nursing supervisor	1		
	Senior staff nurse	9		
	Assistant nurse	1		
	Nurse aide	1		
	Pharmacist	5		
	Lab technician	2		
	Dental tech	1		
	Radiography technician	1		
	Sanitary inspector	1		
	EPI technician	1		
	Statistician	1		
	Store keeper	1		
	Health inspector	1		
	TB/leprosy control assistant	1		
	Med technician EPI1	1		
	Health inspectors			
	Junior mechanics			
	Others:	1		
	Driver	2		
	Cook	Vary		
	Attendant, ward boys, gardener	2		
	Security guards	5		
	Cleaners			

table continues next page

Table A.1   Staff Mix at Upazila Level and Below in the Formal Sector *(continued)*

Facility	Staff—health		Staff—family planning	
Health Subcenter/rural dispensary (except where UHCs exist)	Medical assistant	1		
	Pharmacist	2		
	Health assistant	1		
	Health inspector	1		
Union Health & Family Welfare Center (UHFWC) (except where UHCs exist)			Sub-assistant Community Medical Officer	1
			Family welfare visitor	1
			Family planning inspector (supervising family welfare assistants [FWAs])	1
			Pharmacist	
			MLSS[a]	
Community clinics	Health assistant (3 days)		Family welfare assistant (3 days)	1

Source: World Bank 2010.
Note: Recently, one community HCP was added to the staff of community clinics (CCs), who supervises the other staff and delivers services six days a week from the CC. EPI = Expanded Program on Immunization ; MCH = Maternal and child health; UHC = Universal health coverage.
a. MLSS=Member of lower subordinate staff, usually the office assistants or ward boys.

In the private sector at PHC level, there are traditional healers (faith healers and ayurvedic/unani practitioners), a few homoeopathic practitioners, village doctors (*Palli Chikitsok*), and drugstores in village markets that sell allopathic medicine on demand. This has led to the development of a hybrid structure at the grassroots where there is considerable crossover between public and private elements.

An inventory of training received and services provided by different categories of the informal providers is shown in table A.2. Most of them enter the profession through apprenticeship (for example, drugstore attendants), while those who have some kind of semiformal training, are mostly trained in unregistered, unregulated private sector institutions of dubious quality. The only exception is the CHWs who are trained either by government institutions or by NGOs and have been found to be better in providing rational services including rational use of drugs to some extent (Ahmed, Hossain, and Chowdhury 2009).

Human Resources for Health Production

Organizational Structure

Different organizations belonging to the public and private sectors (for profit and not-for-profit NGOs) are involved in the production of different categories of the health workforce (table A.3). The MOHFW in consultation with DGHS and Directorate of Nursing Services takes decisions for setting up new institutions, introducing new courses, and increasing places for enrollment in institutions for physicians, nurses, medical technologists, and paraprofessionals such as medical assistants. Family Welfare Visitor Training Institutes (FWVTIs) under the

Table A.2 Informal HCPs at PHC Level

Provider	Training	Type of services provided	Sector
Faith healer (*Ojha/pir/fakir*)	n.a.	Nonsecular; based on religious belief	Private
Traditional healer (*Kabiraj*)	Mostly self-trained, but some may have training from government or private colleges of traditional medicine	Ayurvedic, based on diet, herbs, and exercise and so on. Sometimes also combine allopathic medicine such as antibiotics and steroids and so on.	Private
Traditional healer (*Totka*)	Self-trained, combine ayurvedic, unani (traditional Muslim medicine originating from Greece) and shamanistic systems; also use allopathic medicine	Combination of ayurvedic, unani, and faith healing	Private
Village doctors/rural medical practitioners (RMPs); in Bangla *Palli Chikitsok*	Few have one year training from government organizations, which stopped in 1982; majority have three to six months' training from unregistered private organizations	Allopathic	Private
Homeopath	Mostly self-educated, but some possess recognized qualification from government or private homeopathy colleges	Homeopathic	Private
Drug vendor/drug seller; also village "quacks"	No formal training in dispensing; none of them are trained in diagnosis and treatment; some learn treatment through apprenticeship or working in drugstores ("quacks")	Allopathic; in addition to dispensing, they also diagnose and treat	Private
Traditional birth attendants	No training or short training on safe and clean delivery by government/private organizations/NGOs	Assisting normal delivery	Private
Community health workers (health/family welfare assistant, NGO CHWs)	Training on basic curative care for common illnesses and preventive health by government/private organizations/NGOs of varying duration	Allopathic: curative and preventive/ health promotion	Public/private/ nonprofit NGOs

Source: Ahmed et al. 2005.
Note: CHW = Community health worker; NGO = Nongovernmental organization; n.a. = Not applicable.

National Institute for Population, Research and Training (NIPORT)/DGFP is responsible for training family welfare visitors (FWVs) in the public sector.

The Bangladesh Nursing Council provides permission for setting up institutions to train community paramedics in the private sector. For such institutions, bodies of the MOHFW give permission to open an institution or start a course. Permission from respective universities that would offer the degree is also required, particularly for private institutions producing graduates (medical, dental, nursing, and technological). For accreditation and licensing, there are different statutory bodies: Bangladesh Medical and Dental Council for medical and

Table A.3 Categories of Health Workforce with Training Institutes, Admission Criteria, and Duration

Health workforce	Courses	Institution	Admission criteria	Duration	Offered since
Doctors	Bachelors (MBBS)	Medical colleges (public and private)	12 years of schooling with science background + national entrance exam	5 years + 1-year internship	1948
Nurses	Diploma	Nursing colleges attached to medical colleges and district hospitals	12 years of schooling with science background	3 years + internship	2010
	Post Basic BSc		Diploma nursing degree	2 years in-service training	
	Bachelor (BSc)	(public and private)	12 years of schooling with science background	4 years + intership	2008
	Specialized	Specialized hospitals/ institutes (public and private)	Diploma nursing degree	Varies by specialty	
Dentists	Bachelor of Dental Surgery (BDS)	Dental colleges (Public and private)	12 years of schooling with science background+ national entrance exam	4 years + internship	1948
Public health	Master of Public Health (MPH)	NIPSOM, medical colleges, universities (private)	Graduation in any biomedical discipline	12–18 months	1970s
Midwives	Midwifery	FWVTI/NIPORT	10 years of schooling	Nonnurse 18 months; nurse midwifery 1 year	1974
	Midwifery as part of nursing	Nursing colleges attached to medical colleges and district hospitals (public and private)	12 years of schooling with science background	Integrated in Diploma and BSc Nursing	Late 1970s– 2010
	Midwifery course	Private institutes	12 years of schooling	3 years	2012
Medical assistants	Diploma	Training schools (public and private)	10 years of schooling	3 years	1976
Family welfare visitors (FWVs)	Certificate	FWVTI/NIPORT; private institutes	10 years of schooling	18 months	
Community skilled birth attendants (CSBAs)	CSBA	Public and private	Experience in community health work	6 months	2003
Technologists	Diploma	IHT (public and private)	10 years of schooling	3 years	1963
	Bachelor	IHT (public and private)	10 years of schooling	4 years	2011

Source: Ahmed and Sabur 2013.

Note: BSc = Bachelor of Science; FWVTI = Family Welfare Visitor Training Institutes; MBBS = Bachelor of Medicine and Bachelor of Surgery; NIPORT = National Institute for Population, Research and Training; NIPSOM = National Institute of Preventive and Social Medicine; IHT= Institute of Health Technology.

dental graduates, Bangladesh Nursing Council for nurses (of all categories), State Medical Faculty for all categories of medical technologists, and Bangladesh Pharmacy Council for pharmacists.

The Bangladesh Technical Education Board (BTEB), affiliated with the Ministry of Education, also provides permission to private sector institutions to run courses ranging from ultrasonography to nursing, as well as courses for technologists and paraprofessionals. However, MOHFW/DGHS and regulatory bodies do not recognize them. Disputes between these two government bodies persist, and the health workforce continues to be produced by institutions permitted by BTEB. Since there is a shortage of health workers, pass-outs from BTEB-approved institutions are easily absorbed by the private sector. Also, since these institutions are approved by a government body, their nonapproval by MOHFW is generally unknown.

The development of the medical graduate curriculum was driven by the regional concept of need-based and community-oriented reforms in the early 1980s (Majumder 2003). The Centre for Medical Education was established in 1983 as a United Nations Development Programme (UNDP)-funded project to initiate the process. Then the first national curriculum was designed in 1988, which was followed by all medical colleges. In 1992, as part of the Further Improvement of Medical College project, the curriculum was revisited to increase community orientation. The revision was completed in 2002. The latest revision of the curriculum came into effect in 2012.

The first curriculum for diploma nursing was developed in 1991. For BSc nursing, the first curriculum was developed in 2008 (before that it followed the diploma curriculum with little modification). The first Master of Public Health (MPH) curriculum was developed by the National Institute of Preventive and Social Medicine (NIPSOM) and followed by different MPH institutes. Bangabandhu Sheikh Mujib Medical University (BSMMU), an autonomous university, is now responsible for developing the national curriculum.

Uniformity of Curriculum

For some health professionals such as doctors, medical assistants, and BSc nurses, all public and private institutions follow the same curriculum developed by the national or central process. But for some health professionals, there is no uniformity of curriculum. For the MPH course, each of the private universities follows its own curriculum. For most professional courses, the language of instruction is English, which is a problem for nurses, medical assistants, and health technologists, and has been reported in several studies as a barrier for learning (Bangladesh Health Watch 2008).

Career Paths of Doctors and Nurses

Doctors can take postgraduate courses in preclinical, paraclinical, and clinical subjects, with the option to acquire further specialization in two different ways: a postgraduate course or a fellowship.

Formal postgraduate courses offered in different institutions include the two-year diploma, three-year M. Phil, 18-month Master of Public Health (MPH), Master of Transfusion Medicine (MTM), and Master of Medical Education (MMED), and five-year master's programs (surgery, medicine) (table A.4). At first, there was only one institution (Institute of Postgraduate Medicine and Research, now BSMMU) offering postgraduate courses for doctors, but since the late 1990s, a couple of public and private medical colleges started offering these courses. As of December 2011, 2,237 places for postgraduate courses were available.

Fellowship (FCPS—Fellow of the College of Physicians and Surgeons) and membership (MCPS—Member of the College of Physicians and Surgeons) are offered to the doctors through four years of training by an autonomous authority, Bangladesh College of Physicians and Surgeons (table A.5). These options create more opportunities for individual career paths and the production of specialized doctors, but different degrees in the same profession may create some confusion in rules for recruitment and promotion.

Nurses, after passing the diploma course, can undergo a two-year post-basic BSc nursing course as in-service training. In 2004, the BSc was introduced as a four-year graduate course. However, there are few BSc nurses, and out of 171 sanctioned posts of class I nurses, only 2 were filled as of December 2011. Specialized nursing courses like cardiac nursing, rehabilitation and pediatric nursing, junior nursing (midwifery) are offered by institutions in the private sector.

Alternative Medical Care Providers

In a medically pluralistic society like Bangladesh, traditional or indigenous medical systems persist and exert a significant influence by competing with and

Table A.4   Number of Places for Postgraduate Courses Offered by Different Institutions

Name of Institution	MS	MD	M. Phil	Diploma	MPH	MTM	MMED	Total
BSMMU	140	150	70	106	X	10	X	476
22 government institutions	312	360	242	478	185	X	15	1,592
10 private institutions	21	38	15	95	X	X	X	169
Total	473	548	327	679	185	10	15	2,237

Source: Bangladesh Health Bulletin 2012.
Note: X = Not offered. BSMMU = Bangabandhu Sheikh Mujib Medical University; MD = Doctor of Medicine; MMED = Master of Medical Education; MPH = Master of Public Health; M.Phil = Master of Philosophy; MS = Master of Science; MTM = Master of Transfusion Medicine.

Table A.5   Number of Fellowship and Membership Awardees by Year and Category

	FCPS					MCPS				
	2007	2008	2009	2010	2011	2007	2008	2009	2010	2011
Total	172	216	239	288	320	108	79	93	125	118

Source: DGHS 2012.
Note: FCPS = Fellow of the College of Physicians and Surgeons; MCPS = Member of the College of Physicians and Surgeons.

(sometimes) delaying the use of mainstream allopathic medicine. Soon after independence in 1971, the government recognized traditional medicine, keeping in force the Unani, Ayurvedic, and Homeopathic Practitioners Act or 1965. It "realized of late that... traditional practitioners constitute an enormous reserve of manpower that has to be utilized if the health of... population were to be improved through extended coverage of PHC." This is also endorsed in the recent National Health Policy (Government of Bangladesh 2012b). Termed "alternative medical care" (AMC), training for these providers is offered by both government and private institutions. These AMC providers, if passed from government or government-approved institutions, are qualified and allowed to practice the system of medicine in which they are trained. However, there are many institutions not approved by the government, and providers passing out from these institutions are categorized as informal.

Summary Implementation of HRH Policies

Table B.1 Summary Implementation of HRH-Related Government Plans and Policies

Policy/plan	Achievements	Failures	Policy impact	Reasons for nonimplementation
First Five-Year Plan (1973–78) Two-Year Plan (1978–80)	- Significant expansion of health facilities and institutions - Changed orientation of health workers toward community and preventive medicine - Creation of a cadre of domiciliary health workers called family welfare worker (FWW) at the grassroots - Significant increase in the production of doctors	- Production of nurses and para-medics fell below the target	- Production of health workforce to be placed in rural areas - Negligence in producing the support staff - Inappropriate skill-mix took its start	Overattention to the production of doctors and field-level workers led to the underpro-duction of nurses and other support staff
Second Five-Year Plan (1980–85)	- Substantial progress in increasing the number of doctors - Production of medical assistants also surpassed the target - Production and increase of multipurpose health workers for every 4,000 population. - Around 40,000 field-level health and family welfare workers were engaged in delivering various domicili-ary components of PHC	- Shortage of midlevel person-nel particularly in paramedic group (radiographers and dental technicians) was found evident	- Rural health service delivery gained momen-tum through the introduction of domiciliary health and family planning workers - Inappropriate skill-mix started to get a sound footing	Increased number of doctors, medical assistants, and field-level workers were considered critical for ensur-ing the provision of PHC services for the rural poor. This realization overshadowed the requirement for producing other support staff

table continues next page

Table B.1 Summary Implementation of HRH-Related Government Plans and Policies *(continued)*

Policy/plan	Achievements	Failures	Policy impact	Reasons for nonimplementation
Third Five-Year Plan (1985–90)	- Progress was achieved in the field of medical education in terms of increased number of outputs in dental and medical colleges - Nurse training facilities were increased	- Shortage of personnel - Quality of training could not be ensured	- Improved doctor-to-population ratio (1:5546) - Shortage of health workforce - Low coverage of health services	- Complicated recruitment procedure in government service - Insufficient training facilities
Fourth Plan (1990–95)	- Progress achieved in medical and dental education in terms of increased annual output - Nurses training facilities were extended	- No master plan for production of different categories of health workforce was produced during this period - No significant revision in curriculum took place - Paramedical profession failed to draw due attention - Numerous training programs were held with duplications and without coordination	- Doctor-to-population ratio improved - Nurse-to-population ratio improved - Huge backlog was created in training	- Managerial weaknesses for handling the quantitative expansion of the health facilities and the workforce

Source: World Bank, adapted from Osman 2013.
Note: HRH = Human resources for health; PHC = Primary health care.

Economic Analysis for Options to Increase Health Care Providers by 2021

Objectives

The objectives of this analysis are the following:

- Quantify direct costs of human resources policy options based on data collected from different sources.
- Compare costs with existing and foreseen fiscal space in the government of Bangladesh's budget.
- Elicit direct benefits of various human resources options for improving service delivery.
- Provide policy-oriented options to increase the number of health care providers (HCPs) by 2021.

Methods

Analytical Approach

Two sets of data are used for this analysis: human resources data and financial resource data. The human resources (new physicians and nurses) are projected based on financial capacity (not needs). These data are from various sources, including Bangladesh health facility data, public expenditure review, and Human Resources Development dataset. Historical data on government budgets for health are used for predicting financial capacity and funding trends. Human resource needs (number of health care providers, especially physicians and nurses) come from government targets and the recommended nurse-to-physician ratio of the World Health Organization (WHO). These data include salary and allowance, pay scale, government-approved budget for all health workers, number of sanctioned (approved) positions and filled positions for physicians and nurses, future targets set by the government, and production capacity of human resources in the country, particularly physicians and nurses.

The analysis entails a medium-term projection until 2021, given that the government has a focus on goals by 2021, under Vision 2021, and the limited historical data from Bangladesh (limited time points and not up to date) that would result in inaccurate estimates in a long-term projection. In addition, we did not include health technologists in the projection because of data limitations. Instead, we included community health workers (CHWs), but due to limited historical data for CHWs, the trend for nurses is used to project that for CHWs.

The salary and allowance for each physician,[1] nurse, and CHW are calculated by dividing total cost by the number of posts (table C.1). These costs per physician and per nurse data (pay scale) are then used to project the future fiscal threshold for physicians and nurses (the budget allocated each year for recruiting and paying new physicians and nurses). For CHWs, there is only one single data point, for 2013, and this is used to calculate cost per CHW for only that year. The monetary unit used for all budget data is million taka.

To estimate the salary portion allocated for the physician and nurse category from the total budget for all health workers, the total budget for all physicians and nurses in 2013, the latest available data point, is calculated by multiplying the sanctioned number of physicians and nurses by their appropriate salary and allowance scales.[2] The linear regression model is chosen, as traditionally the national budget in Bangladesh is incremental. The regression analyses indicate that the annual salary and allowance for each physician follows the following model: $y = 0.15 + 0.026 * year$ [year = 0 for 2007, year = 1 for 2008, year = 2 for 2009 and so on]; while the model for the annual salary and allowance for each nurse follows the following model: $y = 0.1 + 0.011 * year$. Based on these models, the annual salary and allowance for each physician in 2009 is Tk 0.313 million [$=0.15+0.026*6$]. Similarly, the annual salary and allowance for each nurse in 2009 is Tk 0.167 million [$=0.1+0.011*6$]. The annual salary for CHWs is Tk 0.113 million (as provided by the government). These data indicate that 42.9 percent of total salary and allowance in 2013 was allocated for physicians, nurses, and CHWs (table C.2).[3] This percentage is used to estimate the fiscal threshold for physicians and nurses in the next steps.

Historical data of the total budget, which was allocated for all health workers from 2004 to 2009, are used to project future health budgets in coming years. Our analysis in STATA indicates that the linear model fits the data well [R-Square (R^2)=0.95].[4] The future budget is then estimated using this model: $y = 6192+2169*year$ [year 2003 =0, 2004=1, 2005=2 and so on] (figure C.1).[5]

Table C.1 Salary and Allowance per Physician, Nurse, and CHW per Year

Year	Physician	Nurse	CHW
2007	0.15	0.10	n.a.
2011	0.26	0.14	n.a.
2013	0.31	0.17	0.11

Source: World Bank.
Note: CHW = Community health worker; n.a. = Not applicable.

Table C.2　Cost for Physicians and Nurses/Total Cost for Entire Health Workforce

	Annual salary and allowance per person in 2013	Number of sanctioned positions in 2013	Salary and allowance in 2013	Salary and allowance for physicians, nurses, and CHWs in 2013	Total salary and allowance for all health workers in 2013	% salary and allowance for physicians, nurses, and CHWs in 2013
	(1)	(2)	(3)=(1)*(2)	(4)	(5)	(4)/(5)
Physician	0.313	21,628	6,770			
Nurse	0.167	19,066	3,184	11,967	27,887	42.9
CHW	0.113	17,800	2,011			

Source: World Bank.
Note: CHW = Community health worker.

Figure C.1　Budget for Salary and Allowance for All Health Workers

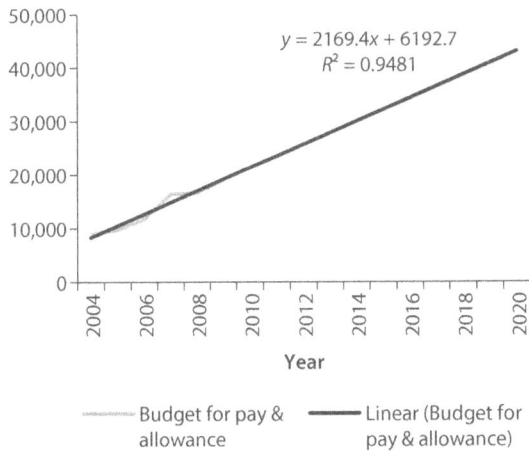

$$y = 2169.4x + 6192.7$$
$$R^2 = 0.9481$$

Source: World Bank.
Note: There are no trend data for CHWs, and thus, CHWs are not included in the trend analysis.

As an example, the projected budget for all health workers in Bangladesh in 2013 would be 6,192+2,169*(2013–2003) = Tk 27,882 million. Bangladesh annual gross domestic product (GDP) growth rate data (World Development Indicators [WDI], accessed May 2014) are also used as a predictor for this projection but did not improve the prediction and were therefore not included in the final model. The fiscal threshold for all health workers is then calculated for each year, adjusting for annual 3.75 percent inflation (table C.3). The fiscal threshold is the amount of budget to recruit new health workers for a certain year. For example, in 2013, the fiscal threshold is estimated at Tk 1,205 million. This was calculated by subtracting 25,713 (projected budget in 2012) from 27,882 (projected budget in 2013) and 3.75%*25,713 (inflation).[6] This means that in 2013 Bangladesh would have about Tk 1,205 million to recruit new health workers. The fiscal threshold for physicians, nurses, and CHWs will be equal to 42.9 percent of the total fiscal threshold for all categories of health workers (based on historical data in table C.2). Details of the fiscal threshold estimation are in table C.3.

Scenarios for Recruiting New Physicians and Nurses Needed through 2021

Based on the fiscal threshold estimated above for physicians and nurses, different approaches to recruiting them are examined. As annual inflation of 3.75 percent has been used in the projection of the fiscal threshold, inflation adjustment for salary and allowance is unnecessary. The latest available salary and allowance scales for physicians and nurses in 2011 are used to project the future budget needed for paying new physicians and nurses under each scenario. The projection of the number of sanctioned positions for physicians and nurses was also used to evaluate against the financial feasibility of each scenario. Production capacity of physicians and nurses in Bangladesh was added to this analysis to evaluate whether the increases of physicians and nurses under each scenario are feasible.[7]

Table C.3 Fiscal Threshold for Physician/Nurse Category and for All Health Care Workers

million taka

Year	Salary and allowance for all health workers (linear regression projection for 2010–21)	Total fiscal threshold for all health workers (this year - last year - last year*3.75%)	Fiscal threshold for physicians, nurses, and CHWs (42.9% of the total fiscal threshold for all health workers)
2004	9,019	n.a.	n.a.
2005	9,760	n.a.	n.a.
2006	11,731	n.a.	n.a.
2007	16,417	n.a.	n.a.
2008	16,658	n.a.	n.a.
2009	19,129	n.a.	n.a.
2010	21,379	n.a.	n.a.
2011	23,548	1,368	419[a]
2012	25,717	1,286	394[a]
2013	27,887	1,205	369[a]
2014	30,056	1,124	482
2015	32,226	1,042	447
2016	34,395	961	412
2017	36,564	880	378
2018	38,734	798	342
2019	40,903	717	308
2020	43,073	636	273
2021	45,242	554	238

Source: World Bank.
Note: Similar to figure C.1, there are no trend data for CHWs; thus, CHWs are not included in this projection. CHW = Community health worker; n.a. = Not applicable.
a. Data include only doctors and nurses at 30.6 percent of the total budget for all types of health workers.

The following scenarios are used to illustrate different approaches for recruiting new physicians and nurses from 2011 to 2021.

1. Laissez Faire (L-F) Scenario[8]

This scenario assumes no additional effort in improving recruitment of physicians and nurses. It lets the current trends take effect into the future. Under this scenario, the numbers of new physicians and nurses are projected using a logarithmic regression. The model for physicians is the following: $y = 10925+935.7*ln(year)$ [2006 as 0, 2007 as 1, 2008 as 2 and so on], and the model for nurse is, $y = 12316+1102*ln(year)$ (figure C.2). Logarithmic regression models are chosen over linear models because they fit the data better (using R^2). In addition, logarithmic models show a slower increase in physicians and nurses than linear models, which seems in line with the recent decreasing trends in filling sanctioned (approved) positions.

2. HRM Policy Scenario: Reaching 2014 and 2016 Targets

The government has set targets for the number of physicians and nurses for 2014 and 2016 (table C.4). Using these targets, the numbers of new physicians and nurses for each year (during 2011–14 and 2015–16) are projected using an averaging approach: the same numbers of new recruitments are set for each year. The starting point of this estimate is the number of filled physicians and nurses in 2010. New recruits of doctors and nurses from 2017 to 2021 are then estimated using the above L-F scenario, which assumes no additional effort in recruitment.

Figure C.2   Projection of the Number of Filled Positions (Laissez-Faire Scenario)

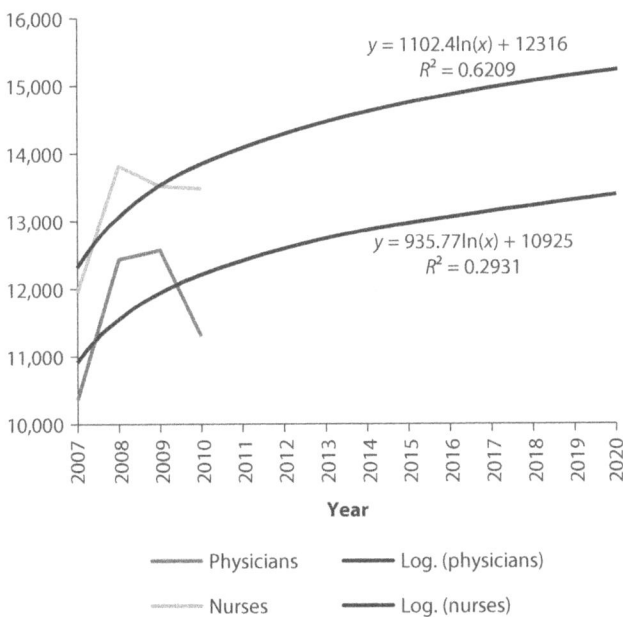

$y = 1102.4ln(x) + 12316$
$R^2 = 0.6209$

$y = 935.77ln(x) + 10925$
$R^2 = 0.2931$

——— Physicians   ——— Log. (physicians)

——— Nurses   ——— Log. (nurses)

Source: World Bank.

The Path to Universal Health Coverage in Bangladesh • http://dx.doi.org/10.1596/978-1-4648-0536-3

Table C.4 Targeted Numbers of Physicians and Nurses

	2014	2016
Physicians	21,700	29,750
Nurses	20,320	25,400

Source: MOHFW 2012.

Because there are no trend data for CHWs, we assume CHWs will grow at a similar rate to nurses. The budget for CHWs, however, is different from that for doctors and nurses, and thus, CHWs are only included in the fiscal analysis below (scenarios I, II, and III).

3. Scenario I: Reaching the Ratio of Physicians: Nurses: CHWs of 1:1:1 by 2021, While Using 100 percent of the Fiscal Threshold for Physicians and Nurses

The numbers of new physicians, nurses, and CHWs to recruit under this scenario are calculated under two conditions: (i) the total cost to pay for physicians, nurses, and CHWs will take up to 100 percent of the fiscal threshold for the whole period 2011–21; and (ii) the physician: nurse: CHW ratio will reach the 1:1:1 target by 2021. The total salary and allowance for physicians, nurses, and CHWs is estimated from the expected number of physicians, nurses, and CHWs multiplied by their appropriate salary and allowance scales.

4. Scenario II and III: Reaching the Ratio of Physicians: Nurses: CHWs of 1:1.5: 1 and 1:2:1 by 2021

These scenarios are examined using the same approach as for scenario I. The only difference is the physician: nurse: CHW ratio, which is set at 1:1.5:1 for scenario II; and 1:2:1 for scenario III by 2021. These scenarios assume using 100 percent of the fiscal threshold for physicians and nurses for the whole period 2011–21.

5. Arithmetic Progression Approach

Instead of keeping the numbers of new recruitment of physicians, nurses, and CHWs fixed every year, we decided to run the projections using an arithmetic approach. In this approach, the future numbers of new physicians, nurses, and CHWs are estimated for the whole period 2011–21. However, the projected numbers of new physicians, nurses, and CHWs to recruit per year are performed using an arithmetic progression. We set their numbers to increase at 15 percent yearly; 2011 figures are used as the starting point. This approach is more practical than recruiting the same numbers every year as it allows the government to adjust, assuming that the total GDP and allocation for health increases every year. In addition, the ratio of filled positions to approved positions shows the current challenges in recruiting physicians and nurses, and thus increasing the target slowly at the beginning is important. This would allow time for policy changes to take effect and infrastructure to be improved—in order to recruit and absorb the many new recruits—and would also allow time for medical and nursing schools to increase production capacity. (Details of the analysis steps are presented in figures CA.1 and CA.2 of annex C.1.)

Analysis and Findings

L-F Scenario

Assuming the recruitment rates stay the same, the L-F scenario results in a very small increase in numbers of physicians and nurses. Only 3,836 physicians are added to the health workforce, versus 44,461 in need (sanctioned positions) (figure C.3a). In addition, this scenario uses only 25 percent of the fiscal threshold for physicians and nurses (figure C.3b), and the nurse-to-physician ratio reaches only 1.14:1 by 2021. This is not a realistic option. Table C.5 gives more detail.

Figure C.3a   Projected Numbers of Physicians and Nurses (Laissez-Faire Scenario)

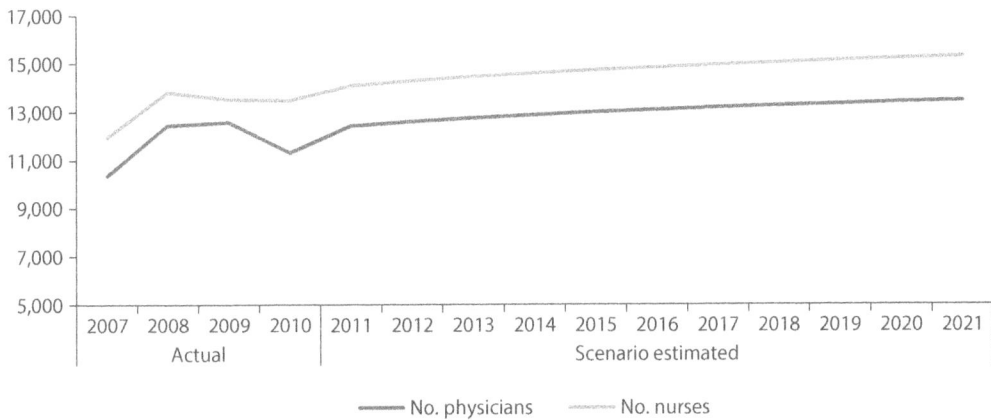

Source: World Bank.

Figure C.3b   Projected Budget for Physicians and Nurses (Laissez-Faire Scenario)

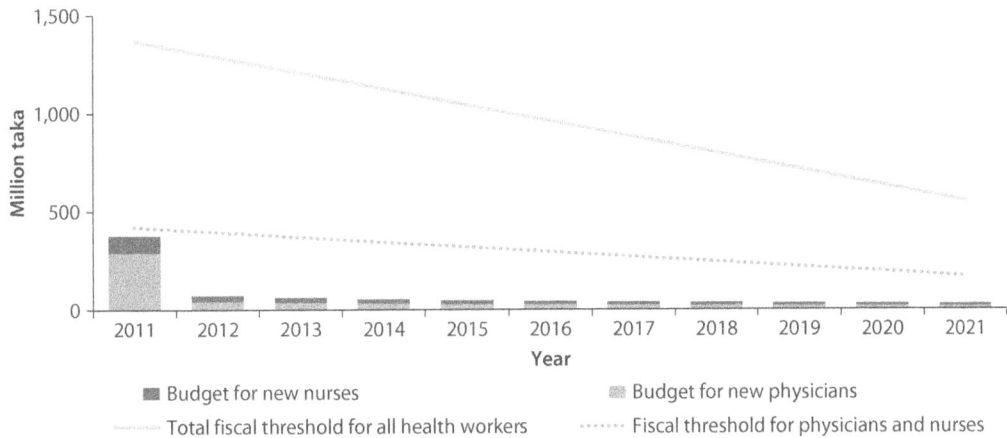

Source: World Bank.

The Path to Universal Health Coverage in Bangladesh • http://dx.doi.org/10.1596/978-1-4648-0536-3

Table C.5 Laissez-Faire Scenario

		Fiscal			L-F scenario (the current trend)					
Year	Fiscal threshold for all health workers	threshold for physicians and nurses	Production capacity: physicians	Production capacity: nurses	No. of new physicians	No. of new nurses	Nurse-to-physician ratio	Budget: physicians	Budget: nurses	Fiscal threshold (%)
2010	n.a.	n.a.	n.a.	n.a.	11,300	13,483	1.19	n.a.	n.a.	n.a.
2011	1,368	419	4,856	1,500	1,131	607	1.13	289.98	87.47	90
2012	1,286	394	4,856	1,500	171	201	1.13	43.74	28.97	18
2013	1,205	369	4,856	1,500	144	170	1.13	36.98	24.50	17
2014	1,124	344	4,856	1,500	125	147	1.13	32.04	21.22	15
2015	1,042	319	4,856	1,500	110	130	1.14	28.26	18.72	15
2016	961	294	4,856	1,500	99	116	1.14	25.28	16.74	14
2017	880	269	4,856	1,500	89	105	1.14	22.87	15.15	14
2018	798	244	4,856	1,500	81	96	1.14	20.88	13.83	14
2019	717	220	4,856	1,500	75	88	1.14	19.20	12.72	15
2020	636	195	4,856	1,500	69	82	1.14	17.78	11.78	15
2021	554	170	4,856	1,500	65	76	1.14	16.55	10.96	16
Total (2021)	**10,570**	**3,237**	**53,416**	**16,500**	**13,459**	**15,300**	**1.14**	**553.55**	**262.05**	**25**

Source: World Bank.
Note: Numbers for 2010 are not new recruits. These are for calculating nurse-to-physician ratio. n.a. = Not applicable.

HRM Policy Scenario

To reach the targets set by the government under the human resource management (HRM) policy, large numbers of physicians and nurses must be recruited in a short time (figure C.4a). This is not feasible because the current recruitment rates are low; the nurse-to-physician ratio would only reach 0.86:1 in 2021, far below the WHO recommendation; and this scenario costs double the total fiscal threshold for physicians and nurses (212 percent) (figure C.4b and table C.6).

6. Scenario I: Physician: Nurse: CHW Ratio of 1:1:1 While Using 100 Percent of the Fiscal Threshold

Scenario I will add 9,212 physicians, 7,029 nurses, and 7,012 CHWs and result in the physician: nurse: CHW ratio of 1:1:1 by 2021 (table C.7 and figure C.5a).

Figure C.4a Projected Numbers of Physicians and Nurses (HRM Policy)

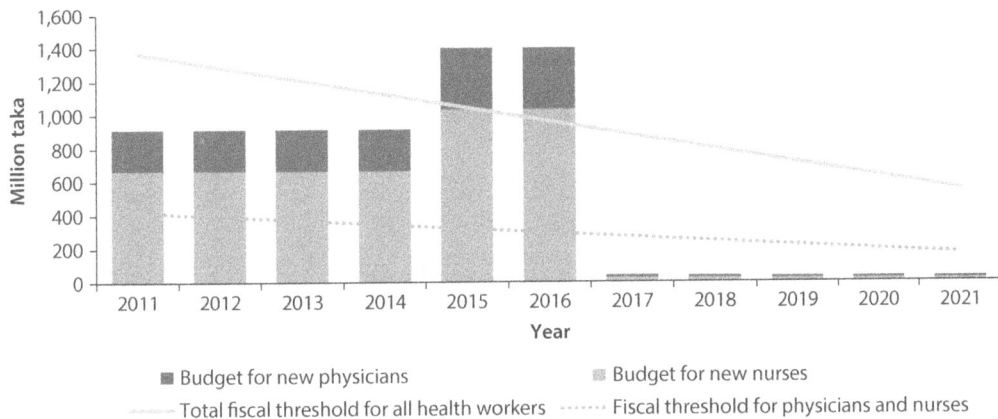

Source: World Bank.

Figure C.4b Projected Budget for Physicians and Nurses (HRM Policy)

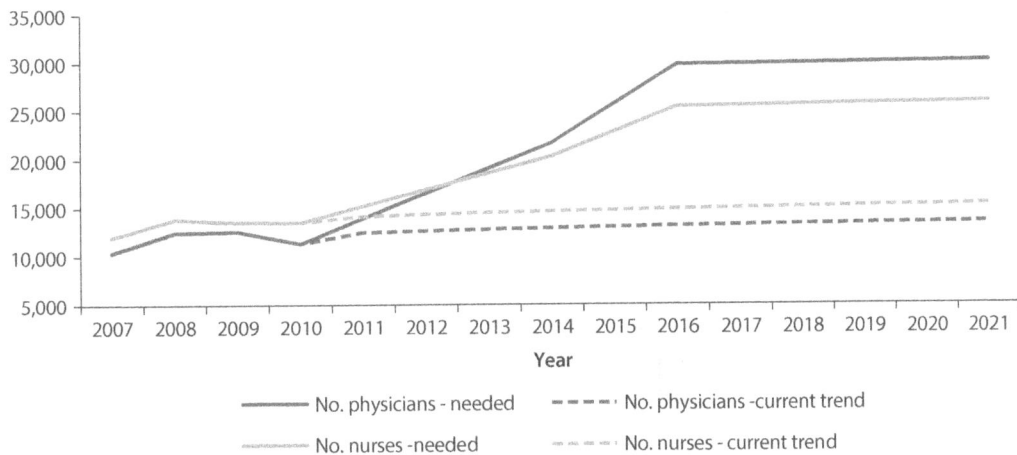

Source: World Bank.

Table C.6 HRM Policy Scenario

Year	Total fiscal threshold: all health workers	Fiscal threshold: old: physicians and nurses	Production capacity: physicians	Production capacity: nurses	No. of new physicians	No. of new nurses	Nurse-to-physician ratio	Budget: new physicians	Budget: new nurses	% (physician+ nurse)/ fiscal threshold
				HRM policy 2014: 21,700 physicians + 20,320 nurses 2016: 29,750 physicians + 25,400 nurses						
2010	n.a.	n.a.	n.a.	n.a.	11,300	13,483	1.19	n.a.	n.a.	n.a.
2011	1,368	419	4,856	1,500	2,600	1,709	1.09	666.64	246.47	218
2012	1,286	394	4,856	1,500	2,600	1,709	1.02	666.64	246.47	232
2013	1,205	369	4,856	1,500	2,600	1,709	0.97	666.64	246.47	247
2014	1,124	344	4,856	1,500	2,600	1,709	0.94	666.64	246.47	265
2015	1,042	319	4,856	1,500	4,025	2,540	0.89	1032.01	366.27	438
2016	961	294	4,856	1,500	4,025	2,540	0.85	1032.01	366.27	475
2017	880	269	4,856	1,500	89	105	0.85	22.87	15.15	14
2018	798	244	4,856	1,500	81	96	0.86	20.88	13.83	14
2019	717	220	4,856	1,500	75	88	0.86	19.20	12.72	15
2020	636	195	4,856	1,500	69	82	0.86	17.78	11.78	15
2021	554	170	4,856	1,500	65	76	0.86	16.55	10.96	16
Total by 2021		3,237	53,416	16,500	30,129	25,847	0.86	4827.86	1782.86	204

Source: World Bank.
Note: Production capacity is from medical and nursing schools in Bangladesh. From 2017 to 2020, recruits are projected using the L-F scenario. HRM = Human resource management; n.a. = Not applicable.

Table C.7 Scenario I: Physician: Nurse: CHW Ratio = 1:1:1 in 2021

Year	Total fiscal threshold: all health workers	Fiscal threshold: physicians, nurses, and CHWs	Production capacity: physicians	Production capacity: nurses	No. of new physicians	No. of new nurses	No. of CHWs	Nurse: physician: CHW ratio	Budget: new physicians	Budget: new nurses	Budget: new CHWs	% fiscal threshold
2010	n.a.	n.a.	n.a.	n.a.	11,300	13,483	13,500	1:1.2:1.2	n.a.	n.a.	n.a.	n.a.
2011	1,368	419	4,856	1,500	479	365	n.a.	1:1.2:1.1	122.69	52.65	0.00	42
2012	1,286	394	4,856	1,500	550	420	n.a.	1:1.2:1.1	141.10	60.55	0.00	51
2013	1,205	369	4,856	1,500	622	475	n.a.	1:1.1:1	159.50	68.45	0.00	62
2014	1,124	482	4,856	1,500	694	529	575	1:1.1:1	177.91	76.34	56.26	64
2015	1,042	447	4,856	1,500	766	584	661	1:1.1:1	196.31	84.24	64.70	77
2016	961	412	4,856	1,500	837	639	747	1:1.1:1	214.71	92.14	73.14	92
2017	880	377	4,856	1,500	909	694	833	1:1.1:1	233.12	100.04	81.58	110
2018	798	343	4,856	1,500	981	749	920	1:1	251.52	107.93	90.02	131
2019	717	308	4,856	1,500	1,053	803	1,006	1:1:1	269.93	115.83	98.46	157
2020	636	273	4,856	1,500	1,125	858	1,092	1:1:1	288.33	123.73	106.90	190
2021	554	238	4,856	1,500	1,196	913	1,178	1:1:1	306.73	131.63	115.34	233
Total		**4,062**	**53,416**	**16,500**	**20,512**	**20,512**	**20,512**	**1:1:1**	**2,361.86**	**1,013.53**	**686.40**	**100**
No. of new recruits					**9,212**	**7,029**	**7,012**					

Source: World Bank.
Note: CHW = Community health worker; n.a. = Not applicable.

The projection lines are under the sanctioned lines, confirming that this scenario is feasible and in line with the government's projected budget for human resources for health (HRH). The fiscal feasibility of this scenario is further confirmed when it will cost 100 percent of the total fiscal threshold (figure C.5b). This scenario will result in recruiting only 10 percent of new graduate physicians and 40 percent of new graduate nurses.

Figure C.5a Scenario I: Projections to Reach a Physician: Nurse: CHW Ratio of 1:1:1 in 2021

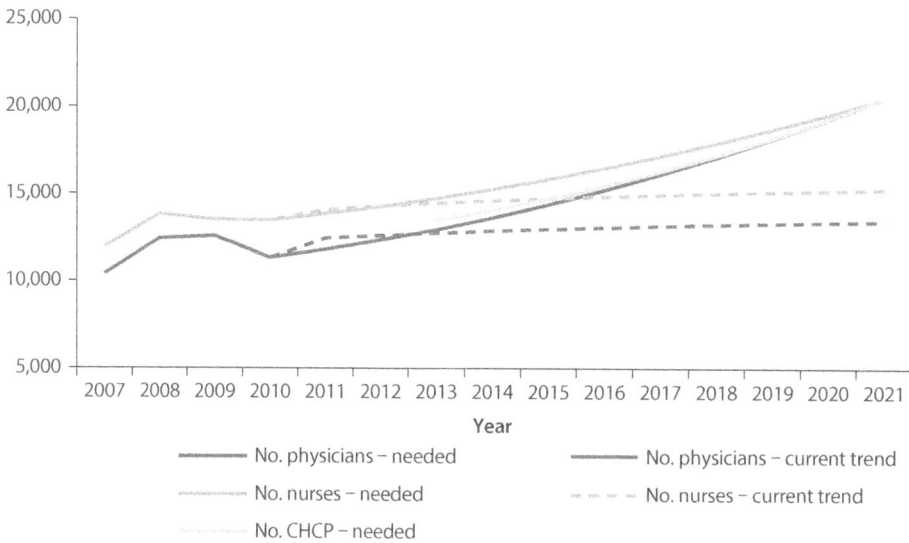

Source: World Bank.

Figure C.5b Scenario I: Budget Projections to Reach a Physician: Nurse: CHW Ratio of 1:1:1 in 2021

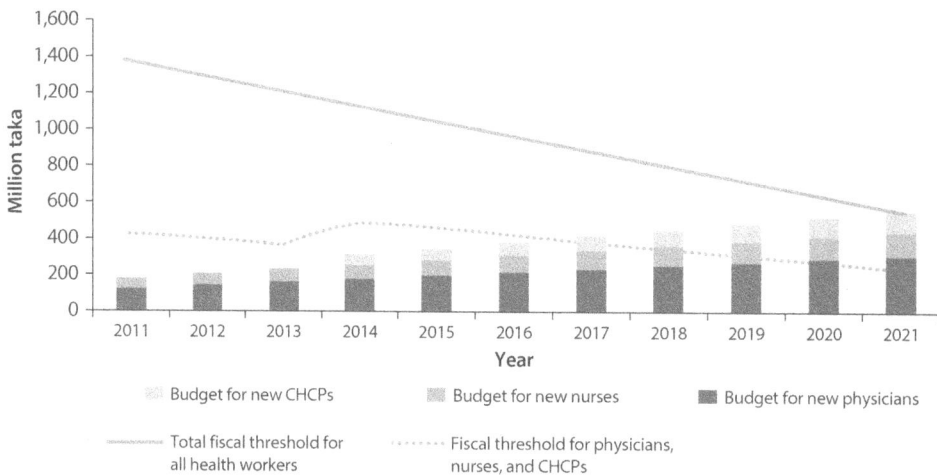

Source: World Bank.

7. Scenario II: Physician: Nurse: CHW Ratio of 1:1.5:1

Scenario II will add 24,436 new physicians, nurses, and CHWs (6,620 physicians, 13,397 nurses, and 4,420 CHWs; table C.8). This will result in the physician: nurse: CHW ratio of 1:1.5:1 in 2021. In addition, the projected lines are under the projected lines for approved positions, confirming the financial feasibility of this scenario (figure C.6a). Figure C.6b also confirms that this scenario will be using 100 percent of the fiscal threshold and absorbing almost all the nursing graduates. However, only about 13 percent of new graduate physicians would be recruited in the period.

8. Scenario III: Physician: Nurse: CHW Ratio of 1:2:1

Scenario III will add 25,355 physicians, nurses, and CHWs (4,609 physicians, 18,336 nurses, and 2,409 CHWs) (figure C.7a). The physician: nurse: CHW ratio of 1:2:1 in 2021 and the recruitment of new nurses and physicians are feasible financially (figure C.7b). However, this scenario will absorb only a small number of medical graduates (only 8 percent of medical graduates will be recruited in 2010–21). In addition, the number of nurses needed exceed the current production trend of about 3,000. In order to adopt this scenario, significant additional funds for recruiting physicians and producing nurses would be required (table C.9).

Discussion

Limitations

The findings and recommendations of this analysis should be interpreted with caution. First, the analysis is based on limited financial and HRH data that were mitigated by performing different regression models and used model fit to choose best models for our projections. Second, as we do not have enough data on future governments' planned budget for HRH for the next 5 or 10 years, we used historical budget data to project the numbers, which may vary depending on the future budget allocation for HRH. Third, the analysis does not include the private health care sector in terms of its capacity to uptake graduates, which will be needed for developing an HRH master plan. Fourth, we project the total number of doctors and nurses needed for the next 10 years based on a limited number of sanctioned (approved) positions of doctors and nurses, which may underestimate actual budget needs. Finally, lack of historical data for CHWs may warrant caution in interpreting projections for them.

Preferred Scenario

Based on the government's fiscal capacity and budget allocation for HRH, scenarios I, II, and III all seem feasible. Table C.10 provides the cumulative number of health workers under the different scenarios. However, scenario II is probably the most feasible as it would absorb more medical graduates and almost all nursing graduates and result in a physician: nurse: CHW ratio of 1:1.5:1.

Table C.8 Scenario II: Physician: Nurse: CHW Ratio = 1:1.5:1 in 2021

Year	Total fiscal threshold: all health workers	Fiscal threshold: physicians, nurses, and CHWs	Production capacity: physicians	Production capacity: nurses	No. of new physicians	No. of new nurses	No. of CHWs	Nurse: physician: CHW ratio	Budget: new physicians	Budget: new nurses	Budget: new CHWs	% fiscal threshold
2010	n.a.	n.a.	n.a.	n.a.	11,300	13,483	13,500	1:1.2:1.2	n.a.	n.a.	n.a.	n.a.
2011	1,368	419	4,856	1,500	344	696	n.a.	1:1.2:1.2	88.17	100.35	n/a	45
2012	1,286	394	4,856	1,500	395	800	n.a.	1:1.2:1.1	101.40	115.41	n/a	55
2013	1,205	369	4,856	1,500	447	905	n.a.	1:1.3:1.1	114.62	130.46	n/a	66
2014	1,124	482	4,856	1,500	499	1,009	362	1:1.3:1.1	127.85	145.51	35.46	64
2015	1,042	447	4,856	1,500	550	1,113	417	1:1.3:1.1	141.08	160.57	40.78	77
2016	961	412	4,856	1,500	602	1,218	471	1:1.4:1	154.30	175.62	46.10	91
2017	880	377	4,856	1,500	653	1,322	525	1:1.4:1	167.53	190.67	51.42	109
2018	798	343	4,856	1,500	705	1,427	580	1:1.4:1	180.75	205.72	56.74	129
2019	717	308	4,856	1,500	757	1,531	634	1:1.4:1	193.98	220.78	62.06	155
2020	636	273	4,856	1,500	808	1,635	688	1:1.5:1	207.20	235.83	67.38	187
2021	554	238	4,856	1,500	860	1,740	743	1:1.5:1	220.43	250.88	72.70	229
Total		4,062	53,416	16,500	17,920	26,880	17,920	1:1.5:1	1,697.31	1,931.80	432.67	100
No. of new recruits					6,620	13,397	4,420					

Source: World Bank.

Note: CHW = Community health worker; n.a. = Not applicable.

Figure C.6a   Scenario II: Projections to Reach a Physician: Nurse: CHW Ratio of 1:1.5:1 in 2021

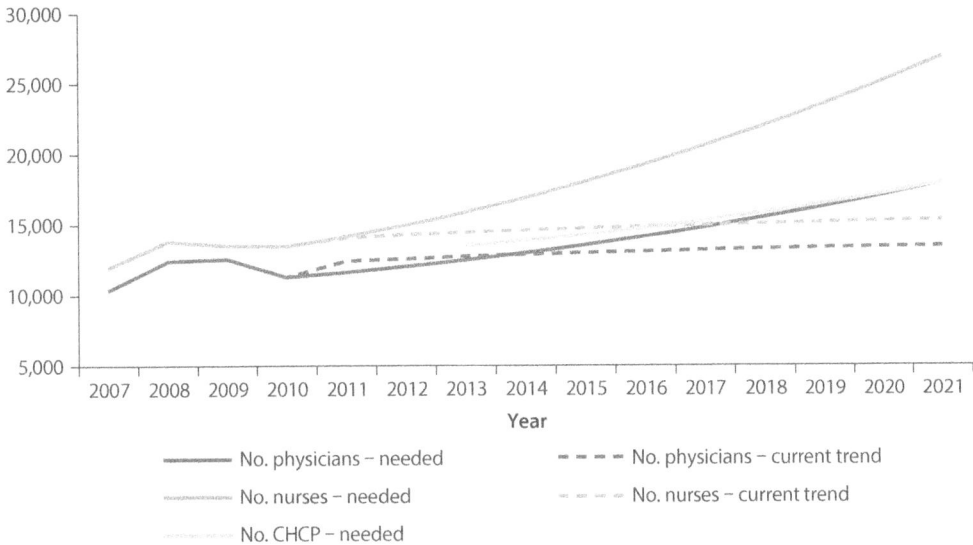

Source: World Bank.

Figure C.6b   Scenario II: Budget Projections to Reach a Physician: Nurse: CHW Ratio of 1:1.5:1 in 2021

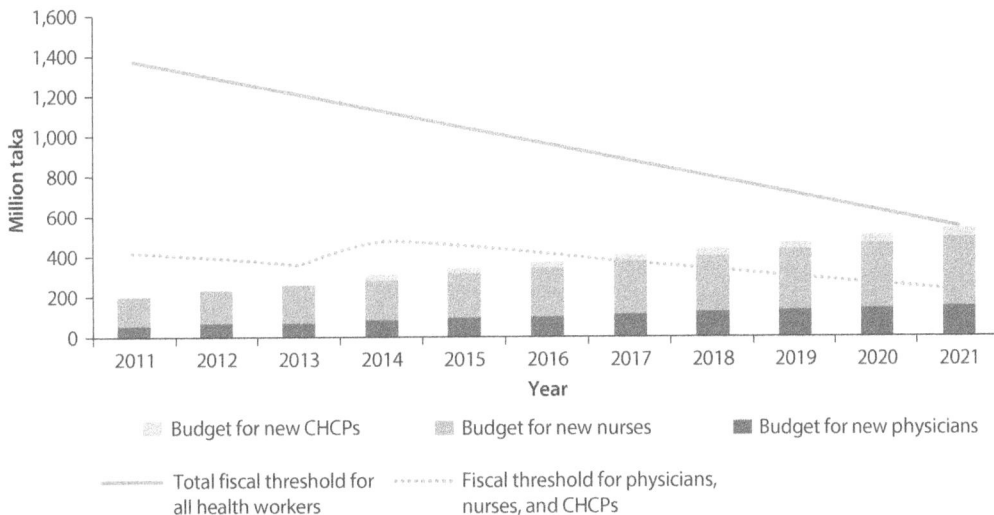

Source: World Bank.

The current rate of production of nursing graduates (1,500 a year) seems to meet needs for new nurses under scenarios I and II, but not III, which requires more. We recommend that nursing schools should increase production capacity of 10 percent a year for the next 10 years, especially if the government aims to reach the nurse: physician ratio of 2:1 (scenario III). At the same time, medical

Figure C.7a   Scenario III: Projections to Reach a Physician: Nurse: CHW Ratio of 1:2:1 in 2021

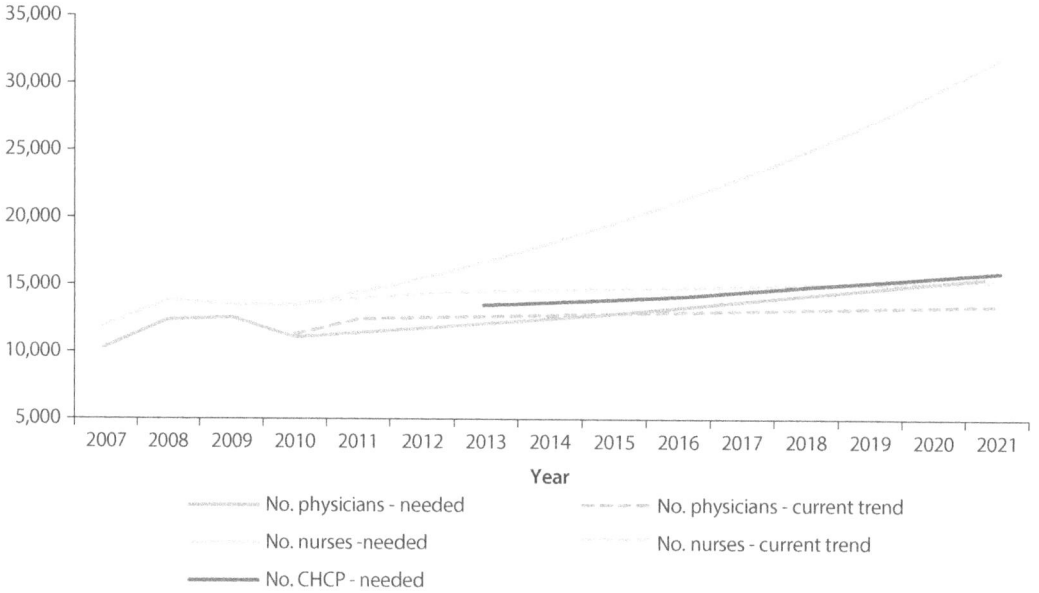

Source: World Bank.

Figure C.7b   Scenario III: Budget Projections to Reach a Physician: Nurse: CHW Ratio of 1:2:1 in 2021

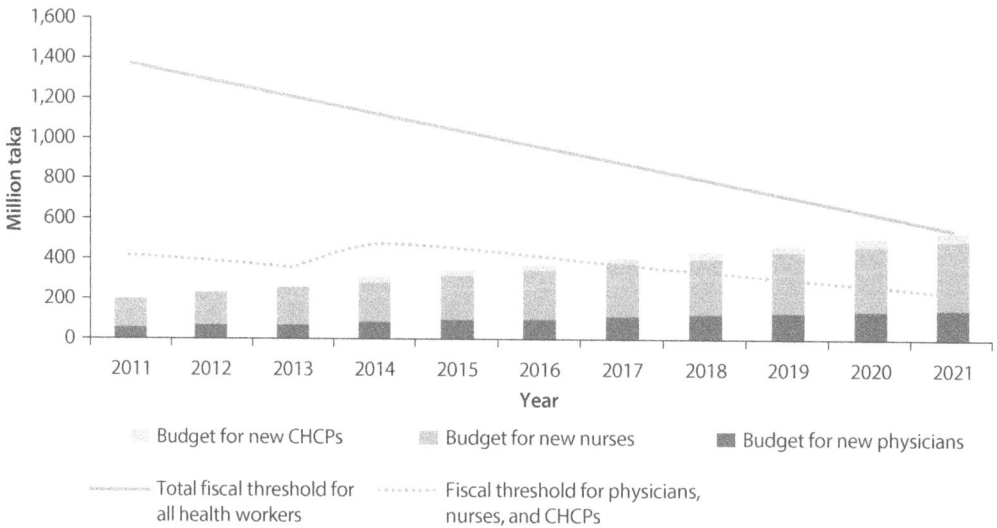

Source: World Bank.

Table C.9 Scenario III: Physician: Nurse: CHW Ratio = 1:2:1 in 2021

Year	Total fiscal threshold: all health workers	Fiscal threshold: physicians, nurses, and CHWs	Production capacity: physicians	Production capacity: nurses	No. of new physicians	No. of new nurses	No. of CHWs	Nurse: physician: CHW ratio	Budget: new physicians	Budget: new nurses	Budget: new CHWs	Fiscal threshold
2010	n.a.	n.a.	n.a.	n.a.	11,300	13,483	13,500	1:1.2:1.2	n.a.	n.a.	n.a.	n.a.
2011	1,368	419	4,856	1,500	239	953	n.a.	1:1.3:1.2	61.40	137.35	n.a.	47
2012	1,286	394	4,856	1,500	275	1,095	n.a.	1:1.3:1.1	70.60	157.96	n.a.	58
2013	1,205	369	4,856	1,500	311	1,238	n.a.	1:1.4:1.1	79.81	178.56	n.a.	70
2014	1,124	482	4,856	1,500	347	1,381	197	1:1.5:1.1	89.02	199.16	19.33	64
2015	1,042	447	4,856	1,500	383	1,524	227	1:1.5:1.1	98.23	219.76	22.23	76
2016	961	412	4,856	1,500	419	1,667	257	1:1.6:1.1	107.44	240.37	25.13	90
2017	880	377	4,856	1,500	455	1,810	286	1:1.7:1.1	116.65	260.97	28.03	107
2018	798	343	4,856	1,500	491	1,953	316	1:1.8:1	125.86	281.57	30.93	128
2019	717	308	4,856	1,500	527	2,096	346	1:1.8:1	135.07	302.18	33.83	153
2020	636	273	4,856	1,500	563	2,238	375	1:1.9:1	144.28	322.78	36.73	185
2021	554	238	4,856	1,500	599	2,381	405	1:2:1	153.49	343.38	39.63	226
Total	**4,062**		**53,416**	**16,500**	**15,909**	**31,819**	**15,909**	**1:2:1**	**1,181.87**	**2,644.04**	**235.87**	**100**
No. of new recruits					**4,609**	**18,336**	**2,409**					

Source: World Bank.
Note: CHW = Community health worker; n.a. = Not applicable.

Table C.10 Cumulative Number of Physicians, Nurses, and CHWs under Different Scenarios

Year	Cumulative number of physicians						Cumulative number of nurses						Cumulative number of CHWs		
	Filled (L-F scenario)	HRM policy	Scenario I	Scenario II	Scenario III	Sanctioned	Filled (L-F scenario)	HRM policy	Scenario I	Scenario II	Scenario III	Sanctioned	Scenario I	Scenario II	Scenario III
2007	**16,461**	**10,365**	**10,365**	**10,365**	**10,365**	**10,365**	**13,275**	**11,950**	**11,950**	**11,950**	**11,950**	**11,950**	—	—	—
2008	**18,280**	**12,435**	**12,435**	**12,435**	**12,435**	**12,435**	**16,478**	**13,815**	**13,815**	**11,950**	**11,950**	**11,950**	—	—	—
2009	**19,243**	**12,573**	**12,573**	**12,573**	**12,573**	**12,573**	**16,595**	**13,519**	**13,519**	**11,950**	**11,950**	**11,950**	—	—	—
2010	**20,234**	**11,300**	**11,300**	**11,300**	**11,300**	**11,300**	**17,183**	**13,483**	**13,483**	**11,950**	**11,950**	**11,950**	—	—	—
2011	20,730	12,431	13,900	11,779	11,644	11,539	18,136	14,090	15,192	13,848	14,179	14,436	—	—	—
2012	21,216	12,602	16,500	12,329	12,039	11,815	18,640	14,291	16,902	14,268	14,979	15,531	—	—	—
2013	21,628	12,746	19,100	12,951	12,486	12,126	19,066	14,460	18,611	14,743	15,884	16,769	13,500	13,500	13,500
2014	21,984	12,871	21,700	13,645	12,985	12,473	19,435	14,608	20,320	15,272	16,893	18,150	14,075	13,862	13,697
2015	22,299	12,981	25,725	14,410	13,535	12,856	19,761	14,737	22,860	15,856	18,007	19,674	14,736	14,279	13,925
2016	22,580	13,080	29,750	15,248	14,137	13,275	20,052	14,853	25,400	16,495	19,224	21,341	15,483	14,750	14,181
2017	22,834	13,169	29,839	16,157	14,790	13,730	20,316	14,958	25,505	17,189	20,547	23,151	16,316	15,275	14,468
2018	23,067	13,250	29,921	17,138	15,495	14,221	20,556	15,054	25,601	17,937	21,973	25,104	17,236	15,855	14,784
2019	23,280	13,325	29,995	18,191	16,252	14,748	20,778	15,143	25,689	18,741	23,504	27,199	18,241	16,489	15,129
2020	23,478	13,394	30,065	19,315	17,060	15,311	20,982	15,224	25,771	19,599	25,140	29,438	19,333	17,177	15,505
2021	23,662	13,459	30,129	20,512	17,920	15,909	21,173	15,300	25,847	20,512	26,880	31,819	20,512	17,920	15,909

Source: World Bank.
Note: Data in bold indicate actual data that are used for the projection; — = Not available (data are not available for CHWs). CHW = Community health worker; HRM = Human resource management; L-F scenario = Laissez Faire Scenario.

The Path to Universal Health Coverage in Bangladesh · http://dx.doi.org/10.1596/978-1-4648-0536-3

schools need not increase—or perhaps should even reduce—the number of new admissions, then closely monitor and adjust the numbers while these policies are implemented.

Given illness and disease patterns in Bangladesh—mainly fever (55 percent), pain (10 percent), and diarrhea (6 percent)—these symptoms and diseases can partly be handled at primary health care level by paramedical assistants or nurses. The cost per nurse is much lower than (only half) that per doctor. These suggest that the right strategy for HRH is to increase nurse production capacity and recruitment.

Distribution of New Recruits by Regions

As recommended above, scenario II is probably the most feasible. We take a further step to deploy the number of new recruits by region for this scenario, taking into account the unbalanced regional doctor: nurse ratios, differing population sizes, and urbanization for each region (table 5.4 in the main text). The number of doctors allocated for a region is proportional to its population size. This number is further adjusted with the current number of doctors per 100,000 population and urbanization. The regions with low doctors per 100,000 population have higher need of doctors and are given higher weights, calculated by the inverse of the current number of doctors per 100,000 population. The more urbanized regions have higher need of doctors and will be given higher weights for calculation. The largest region, Dhaka, is given the highest weight of three, and the smallest region is given the lowest weight of one.

The number of nurses is also proportional to the population size and is further adjusted for the current number of nurses per 100,000 population and urbanization, although the latter is done in the opposite manner of doctors: the less urbanized regions have a higher need for nurses and thus are given higher weights. The distribution of CHWs and adjustment for CHWs is done as for nurses.

Annex C.1:

Figure CA.1   Methodology Used to Determine Scenarios I, II, and III

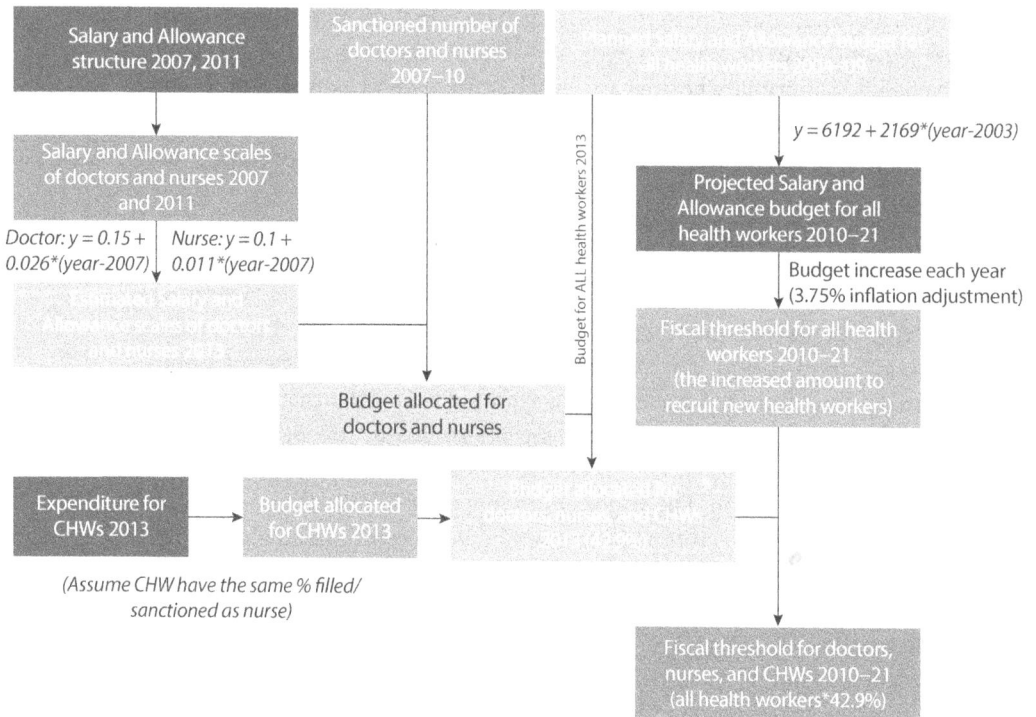

Salary and Allowance structure 2007, 2011

Sanctioned number of doctors and nurses 2007–10

Planned Salary and Allowance budget for all health workers 2010–13

Salary and Allowance scales of doctors and nurses 2007 and 2011

$Doctor: y = 0.15 + 0.026*(year-2007)$ $Nurse: y = 0.1 + 0.011*(year-2007)$

Estimated Salary and Allowance scales of doctors and nurses 2013

Budget for ALL health workers 2013

$y = 6192 + 2169*(year-2003)$

Projected Salary and Allowance budget for all health workers 2010–21

Budget increase each year (3.75% inflation adjustment)

Fiscal threshold for all health workers 2010–21 (the increased amount to recruit new health workers)

Budget allocated for doctors and nurses

Expenditure for CHWs 2013

Budget allocated for CHWs 2013

Budget allocated for doctors, nurses, and CHWs 2010–21

(Assume CHW have the same % filled/ sanctioned as nurse)

Fiscal threshold for doctors, nurses, and CHWs 2010–21 (all health workers*42.9%)

Source: World Bank.

Figure CA.2   Steps in Developing Different Human Resources for Health Policy Options

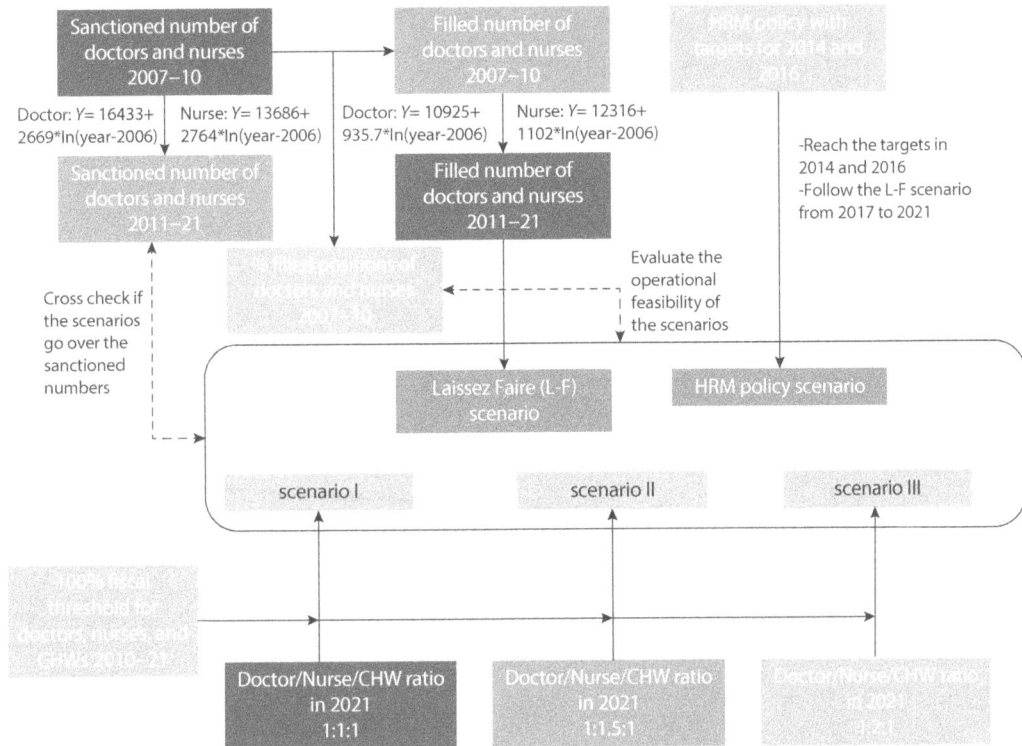

Doctor: $Y= 16433+ 2669*ln(year-2006)$ Nurse: $Y= 13686+ 2764*ln(year-2006)$ Doctor: $Y= 10925+ 935.7*ln(year-2006)$ Nurse: $Y= 12316+ 1102*ln(year-2006)$

-Reach the targets in 2014 and 2016
-Follow the L-F scenario from 2017 to 2021

Evaluate the operational feasibility of the scenarios

Cross check if the scenarios go over the sanctioned numbers

Source: World Bank.

Notes

1. Physicians include medical officers, medical specialists, medical surgeons, and dental surgeons. Nurses include staff nurses and senior nurses.

2. The calculation used 2013 as the latest data point, which is different from (and is more accurate than) the previous analysis that used 2007.

3. The budget for doctors and nurses was calculated at 31 percent, different from the previous analysis of 25 percent because the current analysis used a longer historical data trend; 31 percent also allows for a more meaningful analysis as it gives more room for the production and adjustment of the health workforce.

4. This R^2 indicates that the linear model is a reliable option.

5. In the previous analysis, 2004 was used as 0; 2005 was used as 1, which is inaccurate. The year 2004 must be 1 as this is the first time point in the regression model.

6. A 3.75 percent inflation rate was used, as in the previous analysis from the Ministry of Health.

7. Data from HRD dataset.

8. Because there are no historical data for CHWs, they are not included in this step.

References

Abiiro, G. A., and D. McIntyre. 2013. "Universal Financial Protection through National Health Insurance: A Stakeholder Analysis of the Proposed One-Time Premium Payment Policy in Ghana." *Health Policy Plan* 28 (3): 263–78.

Acerra, John R., K. Iskyan, Zubair A. Qureshi, and Rahul K. Sharma. 2009. "Rebuilding the Health Care System in Afghanistan: An Overview of Primary Care and Emergency Services." *International Journal of Emergency Medicine* 2: 77–82.

Adano, U. 2008. "The Health Worker Recruitment and Deployment Process in Kenya: An Emergency Hiring Plan." *Human Resources for Health* 6: 19.

Adkoli, B. 2006. "Migration of Health Workers: Perspectives from Bangladesh, India, Nepal, Pakistan and Sri Lanka." *Regional Health Forum* 10: 49–58.

Ahmed, M. U., S. K. Islam, A. Quashem, and N. Ahmed. 2005. "Health Microinsurance: A Comparative Study of Three Examples in Bangladesh." Case Study no. 13, CGAP Working Group on Microinsurance Good and Bad Practices, Dhaka, Bangladesh.

Ahmed, N. U., M. M. Alam, F. Sultana, S. N. Sayeed, A. M. Pressman, and M. B. Powers. 2006. "Reaching the Unreachable: Barriers of the Poorest to Accessing NGO Healthcare Services in Bangladesh." *Journal of Health, Population and Nutrition* 24 (4): 456–66.

Ahmed, S. M., and M. A. Hossain. 2007. "Knowledge and Practice of Unqualified and Semi-Qualified Allopathic Providers in Rural Bangladesh: Implications for the HRH Problem." *Health Policy* 84 (2–3): 332–43.

Ahmed, S. M., M. A. Hossain, and M. R. Chowdhury. 2009. "Informal Sector Providers in Bangladesh: How Equipped Are They to Provide Rational Health Care." *Health Policy and Planning* 24 (6): 467–78.

Ahmed, S. M., M. A. Hossain, A. M. R. Chowdhury, and A. U. Bhuiya. 2011. "The Health Workforce Crisis in Bangladesh: Shortage, Inappropriate Skill-Mix and Inequitable Distribution." *Human Resources for Health* 9: 3.

Ahmed, S. M., and M. A. Sabur. 2013. "Overview of the Current State of the Health Workforce in Bangladesh." Unpublished Background Paper, BRAC University, School of Public Health, Dhaka, Bangladesh.

Ahmed, S. M., M. A. A. Majumdar, R. Karim, S. Rahman, and N. Rahman. 2011. "Career Choices among Medical Students in Bangladesh." *Advances in Medical Education and Practice* 2: 51–58.

Ahmed, S. M., and M. M. Khan. 2011. "A Maternal Health Voucher Scheme: What Have We Learned from the Demand-Side Financing Scheme in Bangladesh?" *Health Policy and Planning* 26 (1): 25–32.

Ahmed, T., and S. M. Jakaria. 2009. "Community-Based Skilled Birth Attendants in Bangladesh: Attending Deliveries at Home." *Reproductive Health Matters* 17 (33): 45–50.

Ahmed, S. M., Timothy G. Evans, Hilary Standing, and Simeen Mahmud. 2013. "Harnessing Pluralism for Better Health in Bangladesh." *Lancet* 382 (9906): 1746–55.

Alam, K., J. A. M. Khan, and D. G. Walker. 2012. "Impact of Dropout of Female Volunteer Community Health Workers: An Exploration in Dhaka Urban Slums." *BMC Health Services Research* 12 (1): 260–68.

Alam, K., S. Tasneem, and E. Oliveras. 2012a. "Performance of Female Volunteer Community Health Workers in Dhaka Urban Slums." *Social Science & Medicine* 75 (3): 511–15.

———. 2012b. "Retention of Female Volunteer Community Health Workers in Dhaka Urban Slums: A Case-Control Study." *Health Policy and Planning* 27 (6): 477–86.

Alford, Robert R. 1975. *Health Care Politics: Ideological and Interest Group Barriers to Reform*. Chicago: The University of Chicago Press.

Almond, P., and J. Lathlean. 2011. "Inequity in Provision of and Access to Health Visiting Postnatal Depression Services." *Journal of Advanced Nursing* 67 (11): 2350–62.

Andaleeb, S. 2000. "Public and Private Hospitals in Bangladesh: Service Quality and Predictors of Hospital Choice." *Health Policy and Planning* 15 (1): 95–102.

———. 2008. "Caring for Children: A Model of Healthcare Service Quality in Bangladesh."*International Journal for Quality in Health Care* 20 (5): 339–45.

Andaleeb, S. S., N. Siddiqui, and S. Khandakar. 2007. "Patient Satisfaction with Health Services in Bangladesh." *Health Policy and Planning* 22 (4): 263–73.

Anwar, I., N. Kalim, and M. Koblinsky. 2009. "Quality of Obstetric Care in Public-Sector Facilities and Constraints to Implementing Emergency Obstetric Care Services: Evidence from High- and Low-Performing Districts of Bangladesh." *Journal of Health, Population and Nutrition* 27 (2): 139–55.

Araujo, E. C., and A. Maeda. 2013. "How to Recruit and Retain Health Workers in Rural and Remote Areas in Developing Countries: A Guidance Note." Health, Nutrition, and Population (HNP) Discussion Paper, World Bank, Washington, DC.

Araujo, E. C., A. Mahat, and C. Lemiere. 2014. "Managing Dual Job Holding among Health Workers: A Guidance Note." Health, Nutrition, and Population (HNP) Discussion Paper, World Bank, Washington, DC.

Arifeen, S. E., J. Bryce, E. Gouws, A. H. Baqui, R. E. Black, D. M. E. Hoque, E. K. Chowdhury, M. Yunus, N. Begum, T. Akter, and A. Siddique. 2005. "Quality of Care for Under-Fives in First-Level Health Facilities in One District of Bangladesh." *Bulletin of the World Health Organization* 83: 260–67.

Badr, E., N. A. Mohamed, M. M. Afzal, and K. M. Bile. 2013. "Strengthening Human Resources for Health through Information, Coordination and Accountability Mechanisms: The Case of the Sudan." *Bulletin of the World Health Organization* 91: 868–73.

BBS (Bangladesh Bureau of Statistics). 2011. "Household Income and Expenditure Survey (HIES) 2010." Dhaka, Bangladesh.

Bangladesh Health Watch. 2008. "Health Workforce in Bangladesh: Who Constitutes the Healthcare System? The State of Health in Bangladesh 2007." James P Grant School of Public Health, BRAC University, Dhaka, Bangladesh.

———. 2012. "Bangladesh Health Watch Report 2011: Moving Towards Universal Health Coverage." BRAC University, Dhaka, Bangladesh.

Banu, T., T. K. Chowdhury, M. Kabir, R. Talukder, and K. Lakhoo. 2013. "Bringing Surgery to Rural Children: Chittagong, Bangladesh Experience." *World Journal of Surgery* 37 (4): 730–36.

Baqui, A. H., S. El Arifeen, G. L. Darmstadt, S. Ahmed, E. K. Williams, H. R. Seraji, I. Mannan, S. M. Rahman, R. Shah, S. K. Saha, U. Syed, P. J. Winch, A. Lefevre, M. Santosham, R. E. Black, and P. S. Group. 2008. "Effect of Community-Based Newborn-Care Intervention Package Implemented through Two Service-Delivery Strategies in Sylhet District, Bangladesh: A Cluster-Randomised Controlled Trial." *Lancet* 371 (9628): 1936–44.

Baqui, A. H., S. El Arifeen, H. E. Rosen, I. Mannan, S. M. Rahman, A. B. Al-Mahmud, D. Hossain, M. K. Das, N. Begum, S. Ahmed, M. Santosham, R. E. Black, G. L. Darmstadt, and P. S. Group. 2009. "Community-Based Validation of Assessment of Newborn Illnesses by Trained Community Health Workers in Sylhet District of Bangladesh." *Tropical Medicine & International Health* 14 (12): 1448–56.

Bari, S., I. Mannan, M. A. Rahman, G. L. Darmstadt, M. H. Serajil, A. H. Baqui, S. El Arifeen, S. M. Rahman, S. K. Saha, A. S. Ahmed, S. Ahmed, M. Santosham, R. E. Black, P. J. Winch, and B. P.-I. S. Group. 2006. "Trends in Use of Referral Hospital Services for Care of Sick Newborns in a Community-Based Intervention in Tangail District, Bangladesh." *Journal of Health, Population and Nutrition* 24 (4): 519–29.

Barnett, S., K. Azad, S. Barua, M. Mridha, M. Abrar, A. Rego, A. Khan, D. Flatman, and A. Costello. 2006. "Maternal and Newborn-Care Practices during Pregnancy, Childbirth, and the Postnatal Period: A Comparison in Three Rural Districts in Bangladesh." *Journal of Health, Population and Nutrition* 24 (4): 394–402.

Begum, Khaleda. 1997. "Profile of Postgraduate Doctors." HRD Master Plan 1997. HRD Unit, MOHFW, Government of Bangladesh, Dhaka.

———. 1998. "Evaluation of Framework of Health and Family Planning Personnel System in HRD Master Plan." HRD Unit, MOHFW, Government of Bangladesh, Dhaka.

Berg, A. L., H. Papri, S. Ferdous, N. Z. Khan, and M. S. Durkin. 2006. "Screening Methods for Childhood Hearing Impairment in Rural Bangladesh." *International Journal of Pediatric Otorhinolaryngology* 70 (1): 107–14.

Berlan, D., and J. Shiffman. 2012. "Holding Health Providers in Developing Countries Accountable to Consumers: A Synthesis of Relevant Scholarship." *Health Policy and Planning* 27 (4): 271–80.

Berland, A., J. Richards, and K. D. Lund. 2010. "A Canada-Bangladesh Partnership for Nurse Education: Case Study." *International Nursing Review* 57 (3): 352–58.

Bhatia, M. R., and A. C. Gorter. 2007. "Improving Access to Reproductive and Child Health Services in Developing Countries: Are Competitive Voucher Schemes an Option?" *Journal of International Development* 19 (7): 975–81.

Bigbee, J. L. 2008. "Relationships between Nurse- and Physician-to-Population Ratios and State Health Rankings." *Public Health Nursing* 25 (3): 244–52.

Blum, L. S., T. Sharmin, and C. Ronsmans. 2006. "Attending Home vs. Clinic-Based Deliveries: Perspectives of Skilled Birth Attendants in Matlab, Bangladesh." *Reprod Health Matters* 14 (27): 51–60.

Bollinger, R., L. Chang, R. Jafari, T. O'Callaghan, P. Ngatia, D. Settle, J. McKenzie-White, K. Patel, A. Dossalf, and N. Al Shorbajig. 2013. "Leveraging Information Technology to Bridge the Health Workforce Gap." *Bulletin of the World Health Organization* 91: 890–92.

Bowie, C., T. Mwase, and J. Chinkhumba. 2009. "Health Workers Income and Expenditure in Malawi: An Assessment of the Relative Contribution of Incentive Schemes to Take Home Pay and the Extra Living Costs of Rural Posts." GTZ, Berlin.

Brugha, R., J. Kadzandira, J. Simbaya, P. Dicker, V. Mwapasa, and A. Walsh. 2010. "Health Workforce Responses to Global Health Initiatives Funding: A Comparison of Malawi and Zambia." *Human Resources for Health* 8: 19.

Carlson, C., M. Boivin, A. Chirwa, S. Chirwa, F. Chitalu, G. Hoare, M. Huelsmann, W. Ilunga, K. Maleta, A. Marsden, T. Martineau, C. Minett, A. Mlambala, F. von Massow, H. Njie, and I. T. Olsen. 2008. "Malawi Health Swap Mid-Term Review." *NORAD Collected Reviews* 22.

Chaudhury, N., and J. Hammer. 2004 "Ghost Doctors: Absenteeism in Bangladeshi Health Facilities." *World Bank Economic Review* 12 (3): 423–41.

Chowdhury, A. M. R., A. Bhuiya, M. E. Chowdhury, S. Rasheed, Z. Hussain, and L. C. Chen. 2013. "The Bangladesh Paradox: Exceptional Health Achievement Despite Economic Poverty." *Lancet* 382: 1734–45.

Chowdhury, A. M. R., S. Chowdhury, M. N. Islam, A. Islam, and J. P. Vaughan. 1997. "Control of Tuberculosis by Community Health Workers in Bangladesh." *Lancet* 350: 169–72.

Chowdhury, S., S. A. Hossain, and A. Halim. 2009. "Assessment of Quality of Care in Maternal and Newborn Health Services Available in Public Health Care Facilities in Bangladesh." *Bangladesh Medical Research Council Bulletin* 35: 53–56.

Cockcroft, A., D. Milne, and N. Andersson. 2004. "Bangladesh Health and Population Sector Programme: Third Service Delivery Survey." Community Information and Epidemiological Technologies (CIET), Dhaka, Bangladesh.

Cockcroft, A, D. Milne, M. Oelofsen, E. Karim, and N. Andersson. 2011. "Health Services Reform in Bangladesh: Hearing the Views of Health Workers and Their Professional Bodies." *BMC Health Services Research* 11 (Suppl. 2): S8.

Cockcroft, A., N. Andersson, D. Milne, M. Z. Hossain, and E. Karim. 2007. "What Did the Public Think of the Health Services Reform in Bangladesh? Three National Community-Based Surveys 1999–2003." *Health Research Policy and Systems* 5: 1.

Columbia University, the Earth Institute. 2013. "One Million Community Health Workers —Task Force Report." New York.

Darmstadt, G. L., Y. Choi, S. El Arifeen, S. Bari, S. M. Rahman, I. Mannan, H. R. Seraji, P. J. Winch, S. K. Saha, A. S. Ahmed, S. Ahmed, N. Begum, A. C. Lee, R. E. Black, M. Santosham, D. Crook, A. H. Baqui, and Bangladesh Projahnmo-2 Mirzapur Study Group. 2010. "Evaluation of a Cluster-Randomized Controlled Trial of a Package of Community-Based Maternal and Newborn Interventions in Mirzapur, Bangladesh." *PLoS One* 5 (3): e9696. doi:10.1371/journal.pone.0009696.

Das, Pamela, and Richard Horton. 2013. "Bangladesh: Innovating for Health." *Lancet* 382 (9906): 1681–82.

Dayrit, M. M., C. Dolea, and N. Dreesch. 2011. "Addressing the HRH Crisis in Countries: How Far Have We Gone? What Can We Expect to Achieve by 2015." *Revista Peruana de Medicina Experimental y Salud Pública* 28 (2): 327–36.

DGHS (Directorate General of Health Services). 1997. *Bangladesh Health Bulletin 1997.* Dhaka: Management Information System, DGHS, MOHFW, Government of Bangladesh.

———. 2007. *Health Bulletin 2007.* Dhaka: Management Information System, Directorate General of Health Services, MOHFW, Government of Bangladesh.

———. 2012. *Health Bulletin 2012.* Dhaka: Management Information System, Directorate General of Health Services, MOHFW, Government of Bangladesh.

———. 2014. *Health Bulletin 2013.* Dhaka: Management Information System, Directorate General of Health Services, MOHFW, Government of Bangladesh.

Dolea C., L. Stormont, and J. M. Braichet. 2010. "Evaluated Strategies to Increase Attraction and Retention of Health Workers in Remote and Rural Areas." *Bulletin of the World Health Organization* 88: 379–85.

El-Saharty, S., S. Kebede, P. O. Dubusho, and B. Siadat. 2009. "Ethiopia: Improving Health Service Delivery." Health, Nutrition, and Population (HNP) Discussion Paper, World Bank, Washington, DC.

El-Saharty S., Karar Zunaid Ahsan, Koehlmoos TLP, Engelgau MM. *Tackling Non-communicable Diseases in Bangladesh: Now is the time.* Directions in Development Series, Washington DC, World Bank, 2013 [ISBN: 978-0-8213-9920-0].

Ensor, T., and S. Cooper. 2004. "Overcoming Barriers to Health Service Access: Influencing the Demand Side."*Health Policy and Planning* 19 (2): 69–79.

Evans, T. 2013. "Universal Health Coverage in Turkey: 'Pearls' Emerging from the Pressures of Ambitious Reforms." World Bank, Washington, DC.

Ferdous, J., D. Mamtaz, F. Huda, M. A. Quaiyum, I. Anwar, and M. Koblinsky. 2011. "Are Nurses in Obstetric Wards in Bangladesh Competent Skilled Birth Attendants?" International Centre for Diarrhoeal Disease Research, Dhaka, Bangladesh.

Fogarty, L., and U. Adano. 2009. "The Kenya Emergency Hiring Plan: Results from a Rapid Workforce Expansion Strategy." Capacity Project, Chapel Hill, NC.

Fox, G. J., and Stephanie J. Arnold. 2008. "The Rising Tide of Medical Graduates: How Will Postgraduate Training Be Affected?" *Medical Journal of Australia* 189 (9): 515–18.

Frehywot, S., F. Mullan, P. W. Payne, and H. Ross. 2010. "Compulsory Service Programmes for Recruiting Health Workers in Remote and Rural Areas: Do they Work?" *Bulletin of the World Health Organization* 88: 364–70.

Ghani, A. 2013. *Present State of the Art of Traditional Medicine Practice in Bangladesh.* www. itmrc.org/publication/ch_5.htm (accessed August 30, 2013).

Gil, A., O. Polikina, N. Koroleva, D. A. Leon, and M. McKee. 2010. "Alcohol Policy in a Russian Region: A Stakeholder Analysis." *European Journal of Public Health* 20 (5): 588–94.

Gilson, L., E. Erasmus, J. Borghi, J. Macha, P. Kamuzora, and G. Mtei. 2012. "Using Stakeholder Analysis to Support Moves towards Universal Coverage: Lessons from the SHIELD Project." *Health Policy Plan* 27 (Suppl. 1): i64–76.

Government of Bangladesh. 1980. Second Five-Year Plan (1980–85), Planning Commission, Dhaka.

———. 1990. The Fourth Five-Year Plan (1990–95), Planning Commission, Dhaka.

———. 1998. The Fifth Five-Year Plan (1997–2002), Planning Commission, Dhaka.

———. 2000. "Mid-Term Review of Health and Population Sector Program (HPSP) 1998–2003." Mission Team Report. Planning Wing, Ministry of Health and Family Welfare (MOHFW), Dhaka.

———. 2004. "Program Implementation Plan of HNPSP." Planning Wing, Ministry of Health and Family Welfare (MOHFW), Dhaka.

———. 2008. "Bangladesh Health Workforce Strategy 2008." Ministry of Health and Family Welfare (MOHFW), Dhaka.

———. 2009a. "National Pay Scale 2009." Ministry of Finance, Dhaka.

———. 2009b. "Annual Programme Implementation Report (APIR) 2009" of Health Nutrition and Population Sector Programme (HNPSP), Monitoring and Evaluation Unit, Planning Wing, Ministry of Health and Family Welfare (MOHFW), Dhaka.

———. 2010. *Bangladesh National Health Accounts, 1997–2007*. Health Economics Unit (HEU), Ministry of Health and Family Welfare, Dhaka

———. 2011. "Program Implementation Plan for Health, Population, and Nutrition Sector Development Program (HNPSDP) 2011–2016," Vol.1. Planning Wing, Ministry of Health and Family Welfare (MOHFW), Dhaka.

———. 2012a. "Expanding Social Protection for Health: Towards Universal Coverage Health Care Financing Strategy 2012–2032." Health Economics Unit (HEU), Ministry of Health and Family Welfare (MOHFW), Dhaka; http://www.heu.gov.bd/phocad-ownload/Expanding%20Social%20Protection%20for%20Health%20Towards%20 Universal%20Coverage_Health%20Care%20Financing%20Strategy%20.pdf.

———. 2012b. "National Health Policy 2011." Ministry of Health and Family Welfare (MOHFW), Dhaka.

Gross, J. M., P. L. Riley, R. Kiriinya, C. Rakuom, R. Willy, A. Kamenju, E. Oywer, D. Wambua, A. Waudo, and M. F. Rogers. 2010. "The Impact of an Emergency Hiring Plan on the Shortage and Distribution of Nurses in Kenya: The Importance of Information Systems." *Bulletin of the World Health Organization* 88 (11): 824–30.

Hadi, A. 2003. "Management of Acute Respiratory Infections by Community Health Volunteers: Experience of Bangladesh Rural Advancement Committee (BRAC)." *Bulletin of the World Health Organization* 81: 183–89.

Hadley, M. B., and A. Roques. 2007. "Nursing in Bangladesh: Rhetoric and Reality." *Social Science and Medicine* 64: 1153–65.

Hadley, M. B., L. S. Blum, S. Mujaddid, S. Parveen, S. Nuremowla, M. E. Haque, and M. Ullah. 2007. "Why Bangladeshi Nurses Avoid 'Nursing': Social and Structural Factors on Hospital Wards in Bangladesh." *Social Science and Medicine* 64: 1166–77.

Hamid, S. A., J. Roberts, and P. Mosley. 2011. "Can Microinsurance Reduce Poverty? Evidence from Bangladesh." *Journal of Risk and Insurance* 78 (1): 57–82.

Hamid Salim, M. A., M. Uplekar, P. Daru, M. Aung, E. Declercq, and K. Lönnroth. 2006. "Turning Liabilities into Resources: Informal Village Doctors and Tuberculosis Control in Bangladesh." *Bulletin of the World Health Organization* 84 (6): 479–84.

Hansen, P. M., David H. Peters, Anbrasi Edward, Shivam Gupta, Aneesa Arur, Haseebullah Niayesh, and Gilbert Burnham. 2008. "Determinants of Primary Care Service Quality in Afghanistan." *International Journal of Health Care Quality* 20 (6): 375–83.

Haque, N. A., N. L. Huq, A. Ahmed, and M. A. Quaiyum. 2011. "Community Skilled Birth Attendants: Do They Make a Difference in the Community?" Centre for Reproductive Health Knowledge Translation, Brief no. 2. International Centre for Diarrhoeal Disease Research, Bangladesh (ICDDR,B), Dhaka.

Hasan, J. 2012. "Effective Telemedicine Project in Bangladesh: Special Focus on Diabetes Health Care Delivery in a Tertiary Care in Bangladesh." *Telematics and Informatics* 29 (2): 211–18.

Hatt, Laurel, Ha Nguyen, Nancy Sloan, Sara Miner, Obiko Magvanjav, Asha Sharma, Jamil Chowdhury, Rezwana Chowdhury, Dipika Paul, Mursaleena Islam, and Hong Wang. 2010. "Economic Evaluation of Demand-Side Financing (DSF) for Maternal Health in Bangladesh." In *Review, Analysis and Assessment of Issues Related to Health Care Financing and Health Economics in Bangladesh*. Bethesda, MD: ABT Associates Inc.

Heller, Peter S. 2006. "The Prospects of Creating 'Fiscal Space' for the Health Sector." *Health Policy and Planning* 21 (2): 75–79.

Hipgraved, D., M. Nachtnebel, and K. Hort. 2013. *Dual Practice by Health Workers in South and East Asia: Impacts and Policy Options*. Policy Brief 2 (1). Asia Pacific Observatory on Health Systems and Policies, World Health Organization Regional Office for the Western Pacific Region, Manila, the Philippines.

Hossain, B., and K. Begum. 1998. "Survey of the Existing Health Workforce of Ministry of Health, Bangladesh." *Journal of Human Resources Development* 2: 109–16.

Hossain, M. B., and S. Kippax. 2010. "HIV-Related Discriminatory Attitudes of Healthcare Workers in Bangladesh." *Journal of Health, Population and Nutrition* 28 (2): 199–207.

Hossen, M. A. 2010. *Bringing Medicine to the Hamlet: Exploring the Experiences of Older Women in Rural Bangladesh Who Seek Health Care*. Waterloo, Ontario: Wilfrid Laurier University.

Human Resources Development Unit (HRDU). 1997. "HRD Strategy for Change" (Preliminary Draft), Ministry of Health and Family Welfare (MOHFW), Government of Bangladesh, Dhaka.

ICDDR,B (International Centre for Diarrhoeal Disease Research, Bangladesh). 2005. "Posting of Trained Birthing Attendants: A Comparison of Home- and Facility-Based Obstetric Care." *Health and Science Bulletin* 3 (1): 11–15.

———. 2010. "Doctors with Dual Practice." In Evidence to Policy Series Brief no. 3. Dhaka, Bangladesh.

ICF Macro, Mitra and Associates, and National Institute of Population Research and Training (NIPORT). 2012. "Bangladesh Demographic and Health Survey 2011–2012."

IMED (Implementation, Monitoring and Evaluation Division). 2003. "Health and Population Sector Program (HPSP) Evaluation." Evaluation Wing, IMED, the Ministry of Planning, Government of Bangladesh, Dhaka.

IMF (International Monetary Fund). 2011. "Bangladesh Article IV Consultation." Washington, DC.

———. 2013. "Bangladesh Article IV Consultation." Washington, DC.

IntraHealth. 2009. "Kenya Government Appoints Emergency Health Workers to Permanent Positions." Chapel Hill, NC.

Islam, M. A., S. Wakai, N. Ishikawa, A. M. R. Chowdhury, and J. P. Vaughan. 2002. "Cost-Effectiveness of Community Health Workers in Tuberculosis Control in Bangladesh." *Bulletin of the World Health Organization* 80: 445–50.

Islam, M. T., Y. A. Haque, R. Waxman, and A. B. Bhuiyan. 2006. "Implementation of Emergency Obstetric Care Training in Bangladesh: Lessons Learned." *Reproductive Health Matters* 14 (27): 61–72.

Jenkins, R., R. Kydd, P. Mullen, K. Thomson, J. Sculley, S. Kuper, J. Carroll, O. Gureje, S. Hatcher, S. Brownie, C. Carroll, S. Hollins, and M. L. Wong. 2010. "International Migration of Doctors, and Its Impact on Availability of Psychiatrists in Low- and Middle-Income Countries." *PLoS One* 5 (2): e9049.

JLI (Joint Learning Initiative). 2004. *Human Resources for Health: Overcoming the Crisis.* Cambridge, MA: Harvard University.

Joarder, Taufique, Aftab Uddin, and Anwar Islam. 2013. "Achieving Universal Health Coverage: State of Community Empowerment in Bangladesh." *Global Health Governance* VI (2): p1.

Kamal, N., and M. Mohsena. 2007. "Twenty Years of Field Worker Visitation in Bangladesh: Are They Still Needed?" Population Association of America, 2007 Annual Meeting, New York.

Khan, M., D. Hotchkiss, T. Dmytraczenko, and K. Z. Ahsan. 2012. "Use of a Balanced Scorecard in Strengthening Health Systems in Developing Countries: An Analysis Based on Nationally Representative Bangladesh Health Facility Survey." *International Journal of Health Planning and Management* 28 (2).

Koblinsky, M., I. Anwar, M. K. Mridha, M. E. Chowdhury, and R. Botlero. 2008. "Reducing Maternal Mortality and Improving Maternal Health: Bangladesh and MDG 5." *Journal of Health, Population and Nutrition* 26 (3): 280–94.

Lagarde, Mylene, Andy Haines, and Natasha Palmer. 2009. "The Impact of Conditional Cash Transfers on Health Outcomes and Use of Health Services in Low- and Middle-Income Countries." *Cochrane Effective Practice and Organisation of Care Group* (4).

Lehmann, U., M. Dieleman, and T. Martineau. 2008. "Staffing Remote Rural Areas in Middle- and Low-Income Countries: A Literature Review of Attraction and Retention." *BMC Health Services Research* 8: 19.

Mabud, M. 2005. "Population-Health Interaction Study." Bangladesh Bureau of Statistics, Ministry of Planning, Dhaka.

Mahmood, S. S., M. Iqbal, S. M. Hanifi, T. Wahed, and A. Bhuiya. 2010. "Are 'Village Doctors' in Bangladesh a Curse or a Blessing?" *BMC International Health and Human Rights* 10: 18.

Majumder, M. 2003. "Medical Education in Bangladesh: Past Successes, Future Challenges." *Bangladesh Medical Journal* 32: 37–39.

Maligalig, D. S., S. Cuevas, and A. Rosario. 2009. "Informal Employment in Bangladesh." ADB Economics Working Paper Series, Asian Development Bank, Manila, the Philippines.

Management Information System-Directorate General of Health Services. 2010. "Health Bulletin 2010." Ministry of Health and Family Welfare (MOHFW), Dhaka, Bangladesh.

Mannan, I., S. M. Rahman, A. Sania, H. R. Seraji, S. El Arifeen, P. J. Winch, G. L. Darmstadt, A. Baqui, and B. P. S. Group. 2008. "Can Early Postpartum Home Visits by Trained Community Health Workers Improve Breastfeeding of Newborns?" *Journal of Perinatology* 28 (9): 632–40.

Marmor, Theodore R., and David Thomas. 1972. "Doctors, Politics and Pay Disputes: 'Pressure Group Politics' Revisited." *British Journal of Political Science* 2 (4): 421–42.

May, Maria, Joseph Rhatigan, and Richard Cash. 2011. "BRAC's Tuberculosis Program: Pioneering DOTS Treatment for TB in Rural Bangladesh." Case Study. GHDOnline.

http://www.ghdonline.org/cases/bracs-tuberculosis-program-pioneering-dots-treatme/ (accessed June 14, 2014).

McKenzie, L., and M. Ellis. 2011. "Community-Based Interventions to Improve Neonatal Survival in Low-Resource Settings." *Annals of Tropical Paediatrics* 31 (3): 191–99.

Microcredit Regulatory Authority. 2012. "Microcredit in Bangladesh." Retrieved February 4, 2013, from http://www.mra.gov.bd/index.php?option=com_content&view=category &layout=blog&id=29&Itemid=80.

MOHFW (Ministry of Health and Family Welfare). 2012. "Health Population, and Nutrition Sector Development Program, 2011–16." Government of Bangladesh, Dhaka.

Mohmand, K. A. 2013. "Community Midwifery Education Program in Afghanistan." Health, Nutrition and Population (HNP) Discussion Paper, World Bank, Washington, DC.

Mollik, M. A. H., M. R. Farque, M. O. F. Chowdhury, M. F. Hossain, and M. S. Rahman. 2009. "Peoples Integrated Alliance: Supplementing Bangladeshi Traditional Medical Practice with Western Technologies." *European Journal of Integrative Medicine* 1 (4): 245.

Mridha, M. K., I. Anwar, and M. Koblinsky. 2009. "Public-Sector Maternal Health Programmes and Services for Rural Bangladesh." *Journal of Health, Population and Nutrition* 27 (2): 124–38.

Murphy, C. J. 2008. "Focusing on the Essentials: Learning for Performance." *Human Resources for Health* 6: 26.

Mushtaque, A., R. Chowdhury, Abbas Bhuiya, Mahbub Elahi Chowdhury, Sabrina Rasheed, Zakir Hussain, and Lincoln C. Chen. 2013. "Bangladesh: Innovation for Universal Health Coverage." *Lancet*, November, p. 10.

Namazzi, G., N. Kiwanuka, P. Waiswa, J. Bua, O. Okui, K. Allen, A. Hyder, and E. K. Kiracho. 2013. "Stakeholder Analysis for a Maternal and Newborn Health Project in Eastern Uganda." *BMC Pregnancy and Childbirth* 13 (1): 58.

National Institute of Population Research and Training (NIPORT), MEASURE Evaluation, and ICDDR,B. 2012. "Bangladesh Maternal Mortality and Health Care Survey 2010." Dhaka, Bangladesh: NIPORT, MEASURE Evaluation, and ICDDR, B.

National Institute of Population Research and Training (NIPORT), Mitra and Associates and ICF International. 2013. "Bangladesh Demographic and Health Survey 2011." Dhaka, Bangladesh, and Calverton, MD, US: NIPORT, Mitra and Associates, and ICF International.

Naznin, E., A. Kroeger, N. A. Siddiqui, S. Sundar, P. Malaviya, D. Mondal, M. M. Huda, P. Das, P. Karki, M. R. Banjara, N. Dreesch, and G. Gedik. 2013. "Human Resource Assessment for Scaling Up VL Active Case Detection in Bangladesh, India and Nepal." *Tropical Medicine and International Health* 18 (6): 734–42.

Nguyen, H. T. H., L. Hatt, M. Islam, N. L. Sloan, J. Chowdhury, J.-O. Schmidt, A. Hossain, and H. Wang. 2012. "Encouraging Maternal Health Service Utilization: An Evaluation of the Bangladesh Voucher Program." *Social Science & Medicine* 74 (7): 989–96.

NIPORT (National Institute of Population Research and Training), Mitra and Associates, and Macro International. 2009. "Bangladesh Demographic and Health Survey 2007." Dhaka, Bangladesh, and Calverton, MD: NIPORT, Mitra and Associates, and Macro International.

Noree, T., H. Chokchaichan, and V. Mongkolporn. 2005. "Abundant for the Few, Shortages for the Majority: The Inequitable Distribution of Doctors in Thailand." International Health Policy Program, Nonthaburi, Thailand.

O'Donnell, O., E. van Doorslaer, R. P. Rannan-Eliya, A. Somanathan, S. R. Adhikari, D. Harbianto, C. C. Garg, P. Hanvoravongchai, M. N. Huq, A. Karan, G. M. Leung, C. W. Ng, B. R. Pande, K. Tin, K. Tisayaticom, L. Trisnantoro, Y. Zhang, and Y. Zhao. 2007. "The Incidence of Public Spending on Healthcare: Comparative Evidence from Asia." *The World Bank Economic Review* 21 (1): 93–123.

Osman, F. A. 2013. "Human Resources for Health Policy in Bangladesh: Evolution, Implementation and the Process." Unpublished background paper, Department of Public Administration, Dhaka University, Bangladesh.

Parveen, S., M. A. Quaiyum, A. Afroz, M. Koblinsky, and I. Anwar. 2011. "Improving the Quality of Nurse-Midwives in Bangladesh: Addressing Barriers of Midwifery Course in Diploma and Midwifery Training." International Centre for Diarrhoeal Disease Research, Centre for Reproductive Health, Dhaka, Bangladesh.

Peña, S., J. Ramirez, C. Becerra, J. Carabantesc, and O. Arteaga. 2010. "The Chilean Rural Practitioner Programme: A Multidimensional Strategy to Attract and Retain Doctors in Rural Areas." *Bulletin of the World Health Organization* 88: 371–78.

Peters, D., and R. Kayne. 2003. "Bangladesh Health Labour Market Study." Johns Hopkins University Project Report to Canadian International Development Agency, Baltimore, MD.

Prata, N., M. A. Quaiyum, P. Passano, S. Bell, D. D. Bohl, S. Hossain, A. J. Azmi, and M. Begum. 2012. "Training Traditional Birth Attendants to Use Misoprostol and an Absorbent Delivery Mat in Home Births." *Social Science & Medicine* 75 (11): 2021–27.

Puett, C., J. Coates, H. Alderman, and K. Sadler. 2013. "Quality of Care for Severe Acute Malnutrition Delivered by Community Health Workers in Southern Bangladesh." *Maternal and Child Nutrition* 9 (1): 130–42.

Puett, C., J. Coates, H. Alderman, S. Sadruddin, and K. Sadler. 2012. "Does Greater Work-load Lead to Reduced Quality of Preventive and Curative Care among Community Health Workers in Bangladesh?" *Food and Nutrition Bulletin* 33 (4): 273–87.

Putthasri, W., R. Suphanchaimat, T. Topothai, T. Wisaijohn, N. Thammatacharee, and V. Tangcharoensathien. 2013. "Thailand Special Recruitment Track of Medical Students: A Series of Annual Cross-Sectional Surveys on the New Graduates between 2010 and 2012." *Human Resources for Health* 24 (11): 47.

Rahman, M. M., U. Rob, and T. Kibria. 2009. "Implementation of Maternal Health Financial Scheme in Rural Bangladesh." Population Council, Dhaka, Bangladesh.

Rahman, S. M., N. A. Ali, L. Jennings, M. H. Seraji, I. Mannan, R. Shah, A. B. Al-Mahmud, S. Bari, D. Hossain, M. K. Das, A. H. Baqui, S. El Arifeen, and P. J. Winch. 2010. "Factors Affecting Recruitment and Retention of Community Health Workers in a Newborn Care Intervention in Bangladesh." *Human Resources for Health* 8: 12.

Reed, G. 2010. "Cuba Answers the Call for Doctors." *Bulletin of the World Health Organization* 88: 325–26.

Rowen, T., N. Prata, and P. Passano. 2011. "Evaluation of a Traditional Birth Attendant Training Programme in Bangladesh." *Midwifery* 27 (2): 229–36.

Sack, D. A. 2008. "Achieving the Millennium Development Goals for Health and Nutrition in Bangladesh: Key Issues and Interventions—An Introduction." *Journal of Health, Population and Nutrition* 26 (3): 253–60.

Sarma, H., and E. Oliveras. 2011. "Improving STI Counselling Services of Non-Formal Providers in Bangladesh: Testing an Alternative Strategy." *Sexually Transmitted Infections* 87 (6): 476–78.

Sarr, F. 2010. "Efficiency of Immunization Service in the Gambia: Results of a Stakeholder Analysis." *East African Journal of Public Health* 7 (1): 68–73.

Schmidt, J. O., T. Ensor, A. Hossain, and S. Khan. 2010. "Vouchers as Demand-Side Financing Instruments for Health Care: A Review of the Bangladesh Maternal Voucher Scheme." *Health Policy* 96 (2): 98–107.

Shah, R., M. K. Munos, P. J. Winch, L. C. Mullany, I. Mannan, S. M. Rahman, R. Rahman, D. Hossain, S. El Arifeen, and A. H. Baqui. 2010. "Community-Based Health Workers Achieve High Coverage in Neonatal Intervention Trials: A Case Study from Sylhet, Bangladesh." *Journal of Health, Population and Nutrition* 28 (6): 610–18.

Shiffman, Jeremy, and Yonghong Wu. 2003. "Norms in Tension: Democracy and Efficiency in Bangladeshi Health and Population Sector Reform." *Social Science & Medicine* 57 (9): 1547–57.

Ssengooba, F., S. A. Rahman, C. Hongoro, E. Rutebemberwa, A. Mustafa, T. Kielmann, and B. McPake. 2007. "Health Sector Reforms and Human Resources for Health in Uganda and Bangladesh: Mechanisms of Effect." *Human Resources for Health* 5: 3.

Standing, H., and A. M. Chowdhury. 2008. "Producing Effective Knowledge Agents in a Pluralistic Environment: What Future for Community Health Workers?" *Social Science & Medicine* 66 (10): 2096–107.

Tandon, A., and C. Cashin. 2010. "Assessing Public Expenditure on Health from a Fiscal Space Perspective." Health, Nutrition, and Population Discussion Paper, World Bank, Washington, DC.

Tangcharoensathien, V., S. Limwattananon, R. Suphanchaimat, W. Patcharanarumol, K. Sawaengdee, and W. Putthasri. 2013. "Health Workforce Contributions to Health System Development: A Platform for Universal Health Coverage." *Bulletin of the World Health Organization* 91: 874–80.

Tasnim, S., A. Rahman, and A. K. Shahabuddin. 2009. "Access to Skilled Care at Home during Pregnancy and Childbirth: Dhaka, Bangladesh." *International Quarterly of Community Health Education* 30 (1): 81–87.

UNFPA (United Nations Population Fund). 2011. "State of the World's Midwifery 2011." New York.

USAID (United States Agency for International Development) Bangladesh. 2011. "Bangladesh Health Service Delivery Project: Request for Information Scope of Work." Dhaka.

USC (University of South Carolina) and ACPR (Associates for Community and Population Research). 2012. "Bangladesh Health Facility Survey 2011." Revised Final Report. Dhaka, Bangladesh. http://hpnconsortium.org/admin/essential/Bangladesh_Health_Facility_report_2011_Feb_12_V2.pdf.

Van Doorslaer, E., O. O'Donnell, R. P. Rannan-Eliya, A. Somanathan, S. R. Adhikari, C. C. Garg, D. Harbianto, A. N. Herrin, M. N. Huq, S. Ibragimova, A. Karan, T.-J. Lee, G. M. Leung, J.-F. R. Lu, C. W. Ng, B. R. Pande, R. Racelis, S. Tao, K. Tin, K. Tisayaticom, L. Trisnantoro, C. Vasavid, and Y. Zhao. 2007. "Catastrophic Payments for Health Care in Asia." *Health Economics* 16 (11): 1159–84.

Varvasovszky, Z., and R. Brugha. 2000. "A Stakeholder Analysis." *Health Policy Plan* 15 (3): 338–45.

Vujicic, Marko, Kelechi Ohiri, and Susan Sparkes. 2009. *Working in Health: Financing and Managing the Public Sector Health Workforce*. Washington, DC: World Bank.

Vujicic, M., S. Sparkes, and S. Mollahaliloglu. 2009. *Health Workforce Policy in Turkey: Recent Reforms and Issues for the Future*. Washington, DC: The World Bank.

Werner, W. J. 2009. "Micro-Insurance in Bangladesh: Risk Protection for the Poor?" *Journal of Health, Population and Nutrition* 27 (4): 563–73.

WHO (World Health Organization). 2006. "The World Health Report 2006: Working Together for Health." Geneva.

———. 2010a. "Workload Indicators of Staffing Needs." Geneva.

———. 2010b. "Increasing Access to Health Workers in Remote and Rural Areas through Improved Retention: Global Policy Recommendations." Geneva. http://www.who.int/ hrh/retention/Executive_Summary_Recommendations_EN.pdf.

———. 2012. "Dhaka Declaration. Strengthening the Health Workforce in South-East Asia." Resolution SEA/RC59/R6.

———. 2014. "Bangladesh National Health Accounts."

Wilbulpolprasert, S., and P. Pengpaibon. 2003. "Integrated Strategies to Tackle the Inequitable Distribution of Doctors in Thailand: Four Decades of Experience." *Human Resource for Health* 1: 12.

World Bank. 1993. "World Development Report 1993: Investing in Health." Washington, DC.

———. 2003. "Private Sector Assessment for Health, Nutrition and Population (HNP) in Bangladesh." Report no. 27005-BD. Washington, DC. http://siteresources.worldbank. org/INTBANGLADESH/Data%20and%20Reference/20206318/Bangladesh_PSA_ for_HNP-Full%20report.pdf.

———. 2010. "Bangladesh Health Sector Profile 2010." Dhaka.

———. 2012. *World Development Indicators*. http://data.worldbank.org/country/bangladesh.

———. 2013. *World Development Indicators*. http://data.worldbank.org/country/bangladesh.

———. 2014. *World Development Indicators*. http://data.worldbank.org/country/ bangladesh#cp_wdi.

Zaman, S. 2009. "Ladies without Lamps: Nurses in Bangladesh." *Quality of Health Services* 19 (3): 366–74.

Zurn P., L. Codjia, F. L. Sall, and J. M. Braicheta. 2010. "How to Recruit and Retain Health Workers in Underserved Areas: The Senegalese Experience." *Bulletin of the World Health Organization* 88: 386–89.

Note: The source for all boxes and figures that have "Source: World Bank" is this publication.

Environmental Benefits Statement

The World Bank is committed to reducing its environmental footprint. In support of this commitment, the Publishing and Knowledge Division leverages electronic publishing options and print-on-demand technology, which is located in regional hubs worldwide. Together, these initiatives enable print runs to be lowered and shipping distances decreased, resulting in reduced paper consumption, chemical use, greenhouse gas emissions, and waste.

The Publishing and Knowledge Division follows the recommended standards for paper use set by the Green Press Initiative. Whenever possible, books are printed on 50 percent to 100 percent postconsumer recycled paper, and at least 50 percent of the fiber in our book paper is either unbleached or bleached using Totally Chlorine Free (TCF), Processed Chlorine Free (PCF), or Enhanced Elemental Chlorine Free (EECF) processes.

More information about the Bank's environmental philosophy can be found at http://crinfo.worldbank.org/wbcrinfo/node/4.

green press
INITIATIVE